A Widow's Journal

A Widow's Journal

A New Path, A New Purpose

Kat Timonen

XULON PRESS

Xulon Press
555 Winderley Pl, Suite 225
Maitland, FL 32751
407.339.4217
www.xulonpress.com

Paperback ISBN-13: 978-1-66288-355-2
Ebook ISBN-13: 978-1-66288-356-9

Dedicated

- To the memory of my late husband, Dan, who exemplified Micah 6:8

  "He has told you, O man, what does the Lord require of you but to do justice, and to love kindness, and to walk humbly with your God."

- To my sons, Josh (and Maureen) and Aaron (and Brittany), for standing by me in the darkest hours.

Table of Contents

Foreword

Life changes and transitions can catch us unprepared for what comes next. For probably longer than I can remember, I've loved to journal and have found that the practice of writing helps to link the days and ways of my life. Like scaffolding, writing helps me to process the transitions and new seasons.

Whenever my husband and I travelled, my notebook and Bible were part of my luggage. I'd become committed to scripture journaling over the years, and when we'd flown to Fairbanks, Alaska that summer for the birth of our grandson, my journal was with me. But then Covid got us both. It hit my husband, Dan, especially hard, turning into Covid pneumonia within hours. Hospitalized in the ICU, he lived three weeks. And I became a widow.

I stayed a week longer in Alaska. It was one long, numb week. Somehow, thanks to my sons Josh and Aaron, all the necessary tasks were completed such as funeral home, cremation, and shipping his cremains to Texas. The original goal for Dan and I had been to move to Texas. We'd already sold our home of nearly 40 years in Oregon and had driven to our son's place in Texas. So I would simply do the next thing, I reasoned. I would return to Central Texas. By that time, my own Covid fever was finally gone, and I could travel. Besides, so much in Alaska was triggering the nightmare of the past month. I left Fairbanks on a "red eye" (How ironic is that?! A weeping widow on a red eye!) and arrived at Dallas-Ft. Worth Airport in the early morning hours. I don't recall much about that flight except the Chip Ingram podcasts playing on my headphones. Twenty-four hours later, Saturday morning, Josh said that there's a grief group that meets at church and would I like to go? Still a bit unsure, I decided this was help being offered, so off we went. I felt ragged, numb, and parched, but that group would become a source of hope, connection, and help for us. A few weeks later, they started the Grief Share program. Including Aaron in Fairbanks via Zoom was a good opportunity for us all three to be together every Saturday morning. God provided vital connections during this transition time for what we needed to start this journey.

One thing Grief Share encourages, along with their workbook, is journaling. So, I did. I began to learn that if I were going to find some healing in this loss, I had to choose to trust that the Lord is sovereign, that He is good, and that He would lead me through this valley. Writing about this process would be the start of my healing and the way forward in this new season of life.

So, I began to journal again, but this time with the scriptures that brought comfort. I wrote about the peace He provided when the storm raged within me. Yes, I felt like an amputee, half of me having been ripped away, but verses that reminded me of my wholeness, completeness in Him brought a healing balm. I did not want to sleep, as I feared dreaming about Dan, and having to feel the loss all over again. So, I prayed the Psalms before I fell asleep each night. Many of these Psalms echoed my heart cries and brought peace, which in turn helped bring rest.

I just have to say this: God has been good. He's led me to friendships and fellowship that have helped my healing process immensely. It's also opened my eyes to see that there is such a ministry need for widows in our churches.

Going along this new pathway of widowhood, I have become assured that God still has something for me to do. Since He is the Champion of widows and a Father to the fatherless, He will direct me in His wisdom. I believe He still has a role for me to play in the pathway ahead. It's His new purpose for me. And it appears it involves writing to share with others the comfort, peace, and strength that only He can provide.

If you also find yourself on this path of loss, I invite you to peer over my shoulder at my journal entries as I've started walking this new journey. My prayer is that as you read daily, you will be directed to the only One who can heal our hearts and lead us to the new plan He has set before us in this transition from wife to widow. I hope you will find some balm, some peace, some strength, and comfort in the pages that follow.

Kat Timonen

Journal 1

"Lord, You are my portion and my cup of
blessing; You hold my future." Psalm 16:5

I'm now a widow. A widow. The singularity of that word
sends shock waves that wash over me with grief. Another
widow says these are called ambushes. I'm just figuring out
some of the triggers that envelope me with that sudden chill,
contracting my chest. The chest ache is pretty much constant. Like a dull pain that is with me always. My mouth is
dry. I mean paper dry. No appetite. These are the physical
effects of grief I never knew about.

So it was, I would read this verse like a prayer after a
dear friend, also a widow, reminded me that the Lord is
now my portion. Like the promised inheritance of God's
people, He is my portion. All that is in Him is now available for my desperate needs: His comfort, His strength, His
peace, His help.

He is now my cup of blessing. My cup is my lot in life
and it's God who brings blessings to my current condition.

He fills that cup. I can't expect these benefits from anywhere else. He provides what I need, and I can call on Him over and over. So, if I am to heal from this loss, it will be because the Lord brings peace and comfort. I must learn to rely on Him.

He holds my future. I know this, but when your future doesn't look at all like you thought it would, there are choices to make. Like coming to a fork in the road. I must trust that God is good, that He's sovereign, and that He is in control. He knows the future; I will trust Him to lead me on this new path. My foggy brain means I'll be coming to Him again and again for the strength I need, the wisdom I must have to navigate.

In this time of rearranging banking needs, insurance transfers, car business, it is a comfort to know that I can rely on Him. I won't lie: my cup feels pretty empty. Yet what peace to realize in the middle of the gut-punching pain that God is with me. He cares. He sees me. He knows the wordless prayers my spirit groans in the rising tides of grieving. He will fill my cup. Knowing He holds my future, I can fall back into His arms of Grace. I will make the choice to keep trusting Him Who is my portion, my cup of blessing, and the One who holds my "new" future.

Lord, this is not what I expected. The shock of losing him feels unbearable. I feel like an amputee. I'm missing such a big part of me. But then I remember Who You are, Lord: My portion, my inheritance, my cup of blessing that is full of Your promises. You hold my future for all the days to come. You know the challenges of each one, yet I know You will be with me, never leaving, never abandoning me. And for that, I am thankful. I know I need to sleep, so I put myself into your keeping grace. In Jesus' Name, Amen

Grief notes: The early days of grieving draws disbelief around you like a shawl. Is it true? Yes, my he is gone. His voice, his smile, his laugh, his hugs. Our world is shaken. We have choices to make in these moments. And the journey begins.

Journal 2

"God in His holy dwelling is a father of
the fatherless and a champion of widows."
Psalm 68:5

God can see my every need before I'm even aware
of it. Heartache. Weakness. I'm all too familiar with the
waves of grief that sweep over me in the evening as well
as the morning when I realize anew that Dan's pillow lies
undented. This is reality: I am a widow. This is permanent.
So, I steady myself with God's all sufficient grace. This is
where His Word reassures me: I can continue walking this
journey with Him, for His strength is made perfect in my
weakness. My tentative steps are in His view, as He knows
what lies ahead as well as He knows what's in the past.

For my grown sons and their families, He is father of the
now fatherless. And Grandpa-less. He sees their life needs
and will respond in His unmatched lovingkindness. He
alone can look into the future and see their road ahead, too,
so I will surround them in prayer as well. And yes, I know

He is a champion of widows, and He will defend my cause and handle all the needs I will cast upon Him, because He cares for me. He already knows my days ahead, even from before I was born. It's a real challenge for me to even think of next month, but I'm trusting God.

I know there are so many ways my weary, aching heart could go, but I remember this: God loves me. God is Sovereign. He is Holy-Holy-Holy and His ways and thoughts are higher than my ways and thoughts. So, I will choose to trust the rest of this path, step by step, to Him. Why would I ever choose to walk away from the One Who does all for my good? He sees, He knows, and His acts are righteous. I don't know all the answers to why my prayers were not answered for Dan to recover, but He alone knows, and I have to leave it there. Even in this pain, I recognize that there must be a reason for God's allowing it. Maybe twenty reasons. I just won't know until Eternity. I choose to trust Him with that, too.

So, for now, I will lean on Him for what He has promised: His sufficient grace, His presence with me, His guiding and wisdom. I'll soak my trembling heart and mind in the water of His Word.

Almighty God in His holy dwelling, the throne room of Heaven, has His eye on me, on my family, as Counselor, Defender, Helper, Refuge, Rock, and Savior. The One Who knows my need and my children's needs before I even ask, promises to be our protection and defense in His infinite grace and mercy.

Lord, Your Sovereign plan is more than I can comprehend right now, but I am just leaning in on Your promises, Your grace, and Your strength. Thank You for being a Father to those who've lost their earthly father, and being the Champion of widows. I trust these faltering steps of mine to your care and wisdom. In Jesus' Name, Amen.

> **Grief notes: The fog of new loss envelops our thinking. Life suddenly seems like it is in slow-motion. This is a time to be cautious with tasks like driving or making decisions. Write things down, make lists, ask others for help if you need to.**

Journal 3

"But You, Lord, my Lord, deal kindly with me for Your name's sake; because Your faithful love is good, rescue me. For I am suffering and needy; my heart is wounded within me." Psalm 109: 21-22

Evenings, especially sundown, are painful times, triggering memories of his final days in the hospital when I still could not visit him, and I was still dealing with my own Covid symptoms. Calls would come in at shift changes to let me know how he was doing. And of course, it was evening when that final call came, and we went to say our last good-byes. Evenings now bring waves of panic stealing over me. And in the lonely quiet, the ache of "it's just me" starts settling in. I can feel my aching heart and chest tightening.

Like a gentle hand on my soul, God directs me to the Psalms. So, I pray some Psalms, the ones that speak my heart. "I will bless the Lord Who counsels me, even at night when my thoughts trouble me." Ps. 16:7 In this first month of widowhood, I've highlighted so many of these helpful verses in my Bible. I can sense He is dealing kindly with me, soothing me. He is showing me comfort, providing me with strength, covering me in grace. And faithful love.

I'm realizing that He is a Holy, Sovereign God whose will is done, for He has designed my life and my days. There are no accidents, no surprises, so I humbly acknowledge that His ways, His thoughts trump my feeble plans. I plainly admit I am weak; I need His strength. He brings comfort when I ask, as well as peace and calm to my fevered thoughts. Losing Dan is a gaping wound: "Heal me, Lord!" He is near, as He has promised to be, to the broken-hearted, saving the crushed in spirit.

As I seek what He wants me to do in the days to come, may my heart remember the years and years of answered prayers and the many blessings He has already lovingly poured out on our family. To see our sons walking with Him, I know He is a God Who rescues and has what's best for us. Even in this painful fog of new grief, I'm beginning to realize how deeply and completely I can trust this God of faithful love.

Lord, I am so thankful for Your Word that comforts and counsels me in these crushing moments that make it hard to simply breathe. Knowing You are with me, promising Your constant presence gives me strength for the next step. I inhale your promises like air. Your hand upon my life right now is what keeps me going. I don't know what I'd do without the peace you bring. Thank You, and I trust You like I've never trusted before. But I know that the deep riches of Your grace are unfathomable. So, I am leaning in on You. In Jesus' Name, Amen.

> **Grief notes: So many losses are wrapped up in one loss. These are secondary losses, and daily we are reminded of more and more losses we incurred by the loss of our beloved.**

Journal 4

"I lift my eyes toward the mountains. Where will my help come from? My help comes from the Lord, the Maker of heaven and earth." Psalm 121:1-2

I catch myself watching the sky, searching the clouds, the endless sapphire blue Texas sky. What am I looking for? I know that the Heaven where Dan is is not visible for me. But still I am drawn to that blue expanse above me, vast, awesome, domed wide above me. Like the vast power and provision of my Heavenly Father, the Author of life, and the Sovereign Determiner of death. He who holds life in His almighty hands, yet is faithful, just, and the Justifier of those who come to Him through Jesus.

I look around at all that needs to be done, sorted out, completed. Where will my help come from? Where will my strength come from to overcome this weakness I feel? Where will my comfort come from to dry the tears that so readily fill my eyes as memories surprise me? Where will my wisdom come from when I need to manage accounts, decide when it's time to buy a house, how to deal with the car title, or manage the contents of a storage unit brimming with forty-two years of memories? The air-robbing crush is almost as big as the sky. But I know my God is bigger.

For now, I will deal with today. Right now. I won't borrow worry from tomorrow. I will recall this: "Cast all your anxiety on Him because He cares for you." (1 Peter 5:7) This is the place I can lay down all my sadness. My help from the Lord allows me to throw all that tightens my chest and wrenches my gut onto Him. So, I breathe the prayer, "Help, Lord." And He does.

Yes, my help comes from the Lord—who made the Heavens and the Earth. The Creator of all things through the word of His power (Hebrews 1:3). The blue-sky-over-Texas Creator Who knows my every need even before I do. Who sees me, loves me, provides for me, and will never leave me, never forsake me. The only One Who can truly help today and each of my tomorrows along this new path He's put me on. I will lift up my eyes. Although Central Texas doesn't have mountains, for this Oregon gal, I know what mountains are for. They are for climbing. They are for giving a sense of direction, where you are and where you're going. Yet with mountains come valleys, but Psalm 23 says my Shepherd, my Help, is with me in this dark valley, so I don't need to fear evil. He knows where He's leading me.

Lord, You know my requests—my weakness, my sorrow. Be my strength, my comfort, my peace. Thank you for Your nearness to me and for Your Spirit Who hears and speaks what my heart just can't right now. So, I trust You. I'm leaning in on your faithful love. In Jesus' Name, Amen

> **Grief notes: Triggers are what prompt us to grieve our loss. They may be special songs, household items that carry a memory, or even an item on the shelf at the grocery store your beloved always enjoyed. Tears will come, and that's okay. We are grieving because we loved deeply.**

Journal 5

"Cast your burden on the Lord, and He will
sustain you; He will never allow the righteous to be shaken." Psalm 55:22

It's been a month since Dan passed from this life into
Heaven to be with the Lord. As the chest-crushing, mind-
numbing, heart-aching, mouth-drying effects descended
upon me, I began my journey into loss. I could feel loss like
an amputee who still senses a non-existent limb that aches,
itches, burns. The loss of my life-mate, my "other half", my
companion, began to dawn on me. Waking to being the
only one in the bed, the other pillow undisturbed, and no
one pulling the covers back from my blanket-hogging ten-
dencies. It's just me. There was only one place I knew I had
to go with this lonely void: to the Lord.

As a child, I'd learned 1 Peter 5:7: "Casting all your cares
upon Him, for He cares for you." I had to cast my pain of
loss, the ache of arms no longer reaching to hug Dan, the
absence of a listener, a co-planner, a co-pilot. I had to do

something with this sudden void or multiple losses that would threaten to sink me each morning in the waves of grief. So, hourly, daily, I began to cast, throw, heave, all these heavy moments onto the Lord. I knew I was not strong enough to carry them. That strength would come from the Lord. He will never allow the righteous to be shaken.

And it did. Slowly. In small places, I'd find His presence would bolster my weakness to accomplish a small task. A phone call, an answered email, an account closed, an account opened. Banking, Insurance. All the questions. Answers. Forms. I was being sustained. He maintained my energy, even through the haze of brain fog, I know it's all His strength and His wisdom. It's none of my own doing. I'm so thankful for His amazing sustaining grace!

Thinking about that word sustain, it means to support, maintain, or keep. It's so accurate that the Lord has provided support for each of my steps so far. His Word has been a rich source of encouragement and strength. The Psalms have shown me a deeper sense of understanding in loss, good reminders of His presence, giving me much needed rest, as well as being my shelter in this storm. Every day, I feel He's rescuing me in my time of need through these scriptures. What a blessing to see the promise: He will never allow the righteous to be shaken. "Shaken" means to waver, slip, shake, or fall according to the Hebrew. So, I might quake with these unsteady limbs, but He's got me. He's sustaining me. Always.

Father, Your grace is proving to be sufficient. Your strength is showing up for my weakness. I am thankful I can cast these burdens onto You and You will guide me through these uncharted steps ahead. You know the way forward, so I surrender it all to You to lead and provide wisdom for all that lies before me. With You, I can walk with confidence. Confidence I don't feel right now, but I trust You, Holy, Sovereign Lord. In Jesus' Name, Amen

> **Grief notes: We need to be honest with grief and pain, expressing it and not pushing it aside. Stuffed grief, like an infected wound, will erupt later in inappropriate ways. Take the time to grieve so that healing comes.**

Journal 6

"God, hear my cry; pay attention to my
prayer. I call to You from the ends of the
earth when my heart is without strength.
Lead me to the rock that is high above me,
for You have been a refuge for me, a strong
tower in the face of the enemy. I will dwell
in Your tent forever and take refuge under
the shelter of Your wings." Psalm 61: 1-4

Sometimes grief grabs my breath, knocks my feet
from under me like a sneaker wave. I find myself awash in
remembering and the renewed realization for today: Dan is
gone from this earth. The permanence hits me. My aloneness, my solo-ness aches. There is no one to recall "our"
memories, but they are "my" memories now. I know this
is a downward spiral, and I need a hand up. I need God's
vantage point. Every time despair comes knocking, it is to
Him that I must go.

Like this Psalm, I ask God, "Lead me to the rock that stands higher than me!" I need the Lord's 30,000-foot perspective. I know this life pales in comparison to eternity where Dan is in Heaven, but I am still earth-bound, so I believe that God still has a purpose for me here. I must choose to trust Him for this new life. I tell myself those very words: there is no going back, this is a permanent change that God foreknew, allowed, and now here I am. Yes, I run to that tower He provides, as it's not only a vantage point, but also a haven of rest from the turmoil inside me. So, here in this strong tower I take refuge in the shelter of His wings, His protection, His strength, His peace, and comfort for today. Of course, I will need to rely on this strength for many tomorrows.

Dwelling, abiding in His tent forever, I know I can trust confidently in all that He has in store for me. What seems like my aloneness, He takes it up and carries it for me. He reminds me that He's always been my refuge, always been present. Only now I am not distracted by my complacency and my comfort. Life has changed. Now, I painfully recognize my need for His constant presence, His strength, and peace. Help, Lord. And He does. Even those unrecognizable groans, He is translating and answering them.

I catch my breath again. God's sovereign ways are His perfect will. My will, what I want and my unreliable feelings, will take me off to the ends of the earth where I will lose perspective of my Heavenly Father. In my aloneness, I try not to focus on the voice of the Enemy whose lie says it's only me and my fears. But I turn to praise the Lord that He shows me He has never left me, never will. God has promised to be my refuge. Always and forever—He leads me to that rock that is higher than I, to the shelter of His wings.

Lord, Thank You for keeping me safe in Your strong tower as my refuge and strength until the storm passes. Your presence gives me hope, realizing there is still a purpose for me. Open my eyes, Lord, to what is next. I put all the possibilities into Your hands to guide me. In Jesus' Name, Amen

> **Grief notes: Being ambushed by grief can be that unexpected moment when something reminds us of our beloved. It can be sight, sound, or scent, but it will draw us back to a memory that may trigger tears. If we are venturing where there may be that possibility, it's good to remind ourselves to anticipate an ambush and ask for grace ahead of time! I can also remind myself that my late husband is alive in the presence of God, and that brings comfort.**

Journal 7

"Be gracious to me, Lord, because I am in
distress; my eyes are worn out from frustration—my whole being as well. Indeed, my
life is consumed with grief and my years
with groaning." Psalm 31: 9-10

It's only been a bit over a month, but it seems so long.
Grief makes the days seem longer. The ache, the tears that
spring up at a memory, or even seeing a random drill bit
tucked away in my jewelry. I hear a song from our dating
days playing in a grocery store, and I am ambushed. The
grief rocks me to the core. It's not hard to imagine that life
can be consumed with grief. For the newly widowed, triggers abound. I know I'll have to dig down into my roots of
reliance on God.

My heartache seems to listen to and be influenced by
my fickle feelings, so I tell myself that Dan was not stolen
from me nor was this abandonment. I'd prayed and so many
folks had prayed for his healing, and in the final answer,

God gave His no. This was a sovereign decision of God's Holy plan played out: The Lord knew this moment from before Dan was even born! (Psalm 139:16) And I know in everything, God's purpose will reign. In His compassion, He knew exactly what Dan's passing would bring about in my life, and the lives of our sons. He knew our family would need His presence, turning to Him for comfort, grace, strength, and peace for this new life.

And yes, He knew the distress that would ensue with becoming a widow, as well as the physical and emotional toll the pain of loss would bring my family. So, the Psalmist says, "Be gracious to me, Lord..." David is asking God for mercy and kindness. We will need these as we begin this journey. Ephesians 2:4 reminds us that God is rich in mercy and great love. Lamentations 3:23 calls to mind that His mercies are new every morning, and that He's a God of great faithfulness. How can I not trust the decisions of the Almighty, Holy God? These are moments I have to submit my worries to Him and pray: God, I trust You. There is a reason, maybe many reasons, but the answers lie with You. As for me and my pain, I'm going to trust You anyway and leave the why with You.

I am persuaded by all the ways He's blessed me that I can trust Him to comfort the pain of loss and guide me through His plan going forward with the same precision with which He prepared for the day of Dan's departure for Heaven.

Despite the anguish, I am determined to lean in on His grace, for as David knew where to take his grief, I will carry this to God as well. A God Who sees me, a God who is my Provider, the One who is my Salvation, the God of Peace and of Mercy. This is the soil of my faith where my trust can only grow, rooted securely in Who this Gracious God is.

Lord, I believe that Your Holy way for us is Sovereign, planned by You. Our numbered days are in Your hand. And I pray with the Psalmist, "But I trust in You, Lord; I say, 'You are my God.'" This journey is in Your power, guide me in these new steps. Make the way forward plain as I wait on You to lead me and comfort me. In Jesus' Name, Amen

> **Grief notes: Sometimes grief immobilizes us. Elizabeth Elliot, widow of the martyred Jim Elliot, said many times that what helped her was to "do the next thing". Find simple tasks and do them. Wipe the counter. Water plants. Dust. If you see something small that needs to be done, do it.**

Journal 8

"Let me experience Your faithful love in the morning, for I trust in You. Reveal to me the way I should go because I appeal to You."
Psalm 143:8

I miss jumping in the car to go somewhere—anywhere—any adventure—with Dan. He was always the driver. Across town, or across the US, I looked forward to our adventures. And what a planner he was, too! Not a detail overlooked or left to chance. Oh, how different life is now! Living in a new state, learning to be the driver on new roads and highways, but I'm grateful I'd traveled some of these very highways with him before!

So, today was full of "firsts". God's faithful love was evident today as I ventured into "town". I headed out for the bigger grocery store, kept a business appointment (thanks navigation and Google maps!), and filled my tank with gas (thanks to coaching from my son!). Oh, yes, I am from Oregon, and I'd never filled my own gas tank! I was very aware and appreciative of all the ways God had provided the support I needed! Even these few steps were encouraging me that I can leave fear in the rearview mirror because I'm not traveling alone!

In many ways, I know this new journey will have times when I need "roadside assistance". "Reveal to me the way I should go because I appeal to You." Whether it's driving on my own in new places, or just the newness of a task I've never before faced, I'm trusting the Lord to guide me, and give me peace when the "solo-ness" stings. How I treasure and appreciate all that Dan taught me and I will dearly miss his strengths and talents. But now I must lean in on the Lord's strength, His grace as He leads. I know He will show me how to do this new life as I make my appeals for support and direction.

So, now I can start gaining more confidence in my forays out into the world, trusting in the One Who will never leave nor abandon me. His Holy Spirit certainly comforts me when I start feeling overwhelmed. Each morning I try to start my day by recalling and enumerating His faithful love to me, how He is supplying me with strength and wisdom for the journey, as well as grace for all the new and different changes that come my way. I'm thankful that He already knows the challenges of each new day and each tomorrow, for He goes before me and is beside me, my all-knowing, all-seeing Lord. Gladly I will make my appeal to Him for what I need in the days and the years ahead for He alone knows and holds my future. He will reveal my way.

Lord, I am blessed with Your faithful sustaining grace. Traveling this new path, I'm still getting used to the "solo" part, but I'm realizing that You were with us all those years, and Your presence is with me still! Thank You for guiding me and helping with details I might miss. In Jesus' Name, Amen

Grief notes: A widow discovers so many ways that we had relied on our beloved! Life becomes a series of learning curves as we negotiate new projects and responsibilities. Our workload doubles as we take on chores and repairs we may have never tackled before.

Journal 9

"Turn to me and be gracious to me, for I am alone and afflicted. The distresses of my heart increase, bring me out of my sufferings." Psalm 25: 16-17

Like waves lapping at my feet, moments wash in that remind me how different this life is now; I am no longer part of a "couple". There is a pain, an ache in this new daily ebb and flow of what my heart feels. There is a physical heaviness that weighs me down like lead, my arms function numbly, inhaling aches my chest. "Turn to me and be gracious" and "bring me out of my sufferings" seem light years apart. And yet…

So many of the Psalms penned by David are prayers. There are conversations with God that plead for His help and His attention in times of dire need. Some are petitions for the Gracious Lord to take notice of his immediate situation and provide for him. In grief, these prayers echo my own soul cries to my Heavenly Father. So, I pray them, straight from the pages of the Psalms. I weep through them. Some days, I can only run my finger across the page, but the Holy Spirit knows the words that I trace. And He brings the wave of comfort, peace, and strength that I need. Such deeply amazing and comforting grace.

"I'm alone and afflicted. Distresses increase. Sufferings" is balanced with "Turn to me. Be gracious. Bring me out". David, in his hardship, knew to ask that only One who could help: the Lord. From his shepherd years protecting a flock, he'd seen the Lord's mighty protection, timely provision, and awesome power. This time would be no different. The only One who could act, he trusted would act. Physically he may have been alone, but he also knew the presence of God, so alone had a different meaning. I get encouragement from this. Alone, yet not alone. This lament may speak my heart cry, but I also notice the full weight David puts on his trust in the Lord, because later in verse 21 he states, "For I wait for you." He put full trust in God, and in God's timing.

Yes, this I know: the Lord has been gracious. His sustaining grace has kept me, and I have known comfort as well as peace through His presence. Through His Word, I've been held close since the night of Dan's passing, pressing my soul into His promises to be with me, never abandoned. Through the distresses of my heart, faith increases with each realization that His heart has supplied my strength. Step by step, He is starting this new journey, carving a trail to bring me out of suffering into His new plan, in His way, for His purposes. I am committing to follow where He's leading me.

Lord, The journey is hard work. Uphill, and downhill. But I choose to trust Your plan and Your purpose ahead of me. You will provide sufficient grace for today. When I start borrowing from tomorrow, or trying to bring yesterday into today, my weakness is all I have. So, Your strength, through Your faithful, sovereign, gracious love will be sufficient. Thank You, Lord. In Jesus' Name, Amen

> **Grief notes: Our identity takes a hit with the loss of our beloved. Who am I now? My role has changed. Am I still a mom? Yes. Am I still a grandma? Yes. Our family was founded in the unity of who we were together. So, there is still a continuation of those important roles and values to instill in the next generations.**

Journal 10

"Now the mind-set of the flesh is death, but
the mind-set of the Spirit is life and peace."
Romans 8:6

"Set your mind on things above, not
on earthly things. For you died, and
your life is hidden with Christ in God."
Colossians 3:2-3

I was texting with my sweet sister-in-law the other day.
She'd become a widow six months before I did, and she
mentioned that closing accounts and removing her husband's name from joint titles felt like he was being erased.
That made me think about my own stresses surrounding
those very same tasks. Am I erasing Dan's life? That stunned
me and made my heart ache in a new way. Never! I want
his kind and generous spirit to be remembered! I want his
selfless spirit, his "extra mile" thinking, his working hard
and diligently no matter the task, as well as his talents and

creative MacGyver-like gifts to be what everyone recalls about him!

Then I realized something. It was a kind of an epiphany: those were attributes of Dan, but they were also attributes of the Holy Spirit living within him! Those gifts cannot be erased!

So, when my mind starts down the path of fear, I re-examine my thinking. Is my current mind-set leading to downward-spiral-thinking like despair, despondence, and defeat? Those are all devoid of hope. Instead, I can choose to have my mind governed by the Holy Spirit, focused on life, the eternal and everlasting, on the peace the Comforter gives. "Set my mind" means just that: establish my thinking on things above. Heaven! This is the arena of life and peace because of salvation through the Lord Jesus. What we set our mind to do might last only a few hours, but we have the Holy Spirit residing in each believer! The Helper! The old me died long ago when I accepted Jesus as my Savior and the new me is hidden with Christ in God. What about the old mind set of the flesh/old me? Well, he may try under Enemy orders to derail my thinking, but the Helmet of Salvation protects my mind. I have to learn in this transition time to take those thoughts captive as in 2 Corinthians 10:5!

As I "set my mind", not focusing on the frustration, stressing new situations, or fear of "what now", I recall

God's promise to never leave me. I remember that Jesus said He'd be with me to the end and always. Earthly document changes just show a graduation date. Dan no longer needs insurance, car titles, or banking accounts. He is in the presence of the One who upholds all things, owns all things, and has riches in glory beyond all measure. For now, I'm thankful for the day our names were written down in Glory, for that means I will one day be there as well. And so, I'll keep my thinking fixed on Him, life and peace, where my life is hidden in Christ.

Lord, You provide life and peace of mind through Your Holy Spirit, the Helper we need every day. Help me set my mind on things above as you lead me forward in service to You. In Jesus' Name, Amen.

> **Grief notes: Loss brings with it a lot of paperwork, phone calls, and notifications to maneuver. Even through the fog and pain, we have important steps to take for the responsibilities of life going on. Be sure to keep a tablet with important dates and numbers as well as when each**

was contacted. A brief description of the conversation, with whom you spoke, and any critical details will help you later recall important information.

Journal 11

"The Lord is the One who will go before you. He will be with you; He will not leave you nor abandon you. Do not be afraid or discouraged." Deuteronomy 31:8

This was a critical time for the Children of Israel: Moses was dying, he would not be entering the Promised Land with them, and they would be looking to Joshua as their new leader. Moses gave specific detail regarding their path forward: the Lord will cross the Jordan ahead of you, He will destroy the nations before you, and you would drive them out, the Lord will deliver them into your hands, do exactly as I have commanded you, be strong, be courageous, don't be terrified or afraid of them, the Lord is the One who will go before you—never leaving nor abandoning you. That must've put some rebar in the spines of these weary travelers. There are many days now that I turn to this account to draw strength from this well: "The Lord is the One who will go before you…be with you…not leave you…abandon you. Don't be afraid or discouraged." As for the nations they were to oust, God would destroy them, and hand the victory over to the Children of Israel. Their job was to be strong, not terrified, and remember what the Lord could do, because He was with them. There's a lesson for me here.

I know the Promised Land lies ahead in this new life and like those looking to Joshua, I can't foresee how to ford the river yet. Then I notice that Joshua simply follows the commands: the priests carrying the Ark of the Covenant, the Presence of the Lord, stepping toward the overflowing water of harvest season, and immediately there is a miracle. Not only do the waters divide, creating a path, but the ground is dry and they step with fearless faith into their next season.

My God knows how to turn a muddy riverbed into a dry path for travelling! Certainly, He will make a way for me, His presence leading, guiding, providing in this new season. I see that His promise of helping them deal with the nations depended on their obedience, so I will pay attention to His directions for me. Don't be afraid or discouraged: that's a command. I am with you: that's a promise. He knows what I'll need, so I will have faith in how He'll provide it.

It would be easy to cave into fear, listen to the Enemy lies, so how do I walk this new path? I recognize His presence is a precious promise of an eternally faithful Promise-keeper. I remind myself: Do not be afraid. God can, and will, handle this loneliness, those memory ambushes that hit me in a chest-crushing electric shock. New responsibilities, financial questions, my "what should I do?" moments. Do not be discouraged. My mind can go there in a split second when I start focusing on details out of my control! There's no altering God's plan. Not a bit. So, I lift my eyes, my mindset, to Him. He is, and was, before me, beside me. Always. No leaving. No fear, no discouragement. Even when the Enemy whispers lies, "You can't do this. It's so unfair!" I know the Lord is with me. With my family. He is the God of the new path, the new way forward, taking me forward toward His new purpose through His faithful promises.

Lord, You promise to be with me and You already see what is before me even if it seems impossible. You alone can make a path where there is no path. Thank You for Your abiding presence and Your power to create the way I am to go. In Jesus' Name, Amen.

> **Grief notes: There is nothing predictable or linear about going through grief. There are not prescribed stages to walk neatly through, and then it's over and**

done. Grief is there. Some days will be sadness and loss, anger and despair or guilt and shame. Some days you move about like you are encased in gelatin, like slow motion.

Journal 12

"This is my comfort in my affliction: Your promise has given me life." Psalm 119:50

In the days that I have walked through so far with loss and grief, I really don't know where I'd be if it were not for the Lord. From the start of Dan's hospitalization, the three weeks of ups and downs of ICU, to the night he passed, the Lord has been my constant source of help and consolation.

I know His strength has been carrying me. In those initial days of constant tears, chest-aching heaviness, the had-to-be-done phone calls, the Lord held me. His Word was always open, praying through tears the laments of the Psalms and praying the promises. The Holy Spirit, my Comforter, would remind me of verses: He will never leave nor forsake me. He is near the broken hearted, saving those crushed in spirit. He is our refuge and strength, a helper who is always found in times of trouble. Even Jesus' words in Matthew 28, "I am with you always to the end of the age." These promises have given so much hope, walking me through this passage to the new season the Lord has for me. The changes are so dizzying at times that my head spins and my heart can barely keep up or know what to do next.

And yes, the grief surges still roll, some being more electric and shocking than oceanic and rolling over me. But I have come to learn this: grief is the price we pay for loving someone. When this one-flesh union is torn from the other, the pain of losing all the identities and roles takes some time to unfold and settle in as fact. I heard someone say it's like an onion: we realize the losses layer by layer. New realizations of loss bring pain anew to the sting of losing our loved one. I believe it's a grace of God that we don't realize it all at once, but little by little, we come to understand each unfolding loss. From the numbness and fog to every morning awaking to remind ourselves that this is the new normal, God allows us to gradually see that there will be a path forward. That there is life. That there is hope and He will walk as guide and counsel with us.

So, in this affliction of grief, there is a comfort to be had: the promises of God have given me life. With the layers of grief, there are layers of healing coming, too: life and hope. The promises of His Holy Spirit comfort me as He hears each cry for help, He sees my soul's need for peace, and He brings verses to mind that were tucked away in my memory. I highlight them now, making them even easier to revisit.

Psalms that speak of shelter, refuge, and the secret place of the Most High remind me He is not only giving me life, but He is also preserving me in this Valley. What an incredible comfort to know there is yet life and hope, there can be a future and a productive purpose down this road. I know it won't be under my power and effort, but Christ in me.

Yes, the path forward is lined with His promises for a new season, new purpose, a continuation of a loving God's sovereign plan. I'm still His child, He is still in control. His promises still give comfort, hope, and life.

Lord, Your promises give me life a reassuring comfort that promises a purpose in this pain of loss. Thank You for the hourly and strength as well as the help that comes from You. I pray I can share this hope and comfort with others in the same way You have blessed me. In Jesus' Name, Amen

> **Grief notes: There are many physical symptoms of grief like the crushing hollow chest feeling, body aches, loss of appetite, hair loss, and even dry mouth. We were not originally created for death; we were made for eternal life.**

Journal 13

"For I am the Lord your God who holds
your right hand, who says to you, 'Do not
fear, I will help you." Isaiah 41:13

I drove into town yesterday to shop for some Fall clothes.
I realized it's hard to gauge how difficult a task will be before
doing it. I thought just the newness of driving into town
would be a challenge, but what I didn't calculate was the
impact of buying or trying to buy new clothes. I began to
think: Who cares?! There's no one to show my purchases to,
no one to model them for or who would give an opinion!
This hit me hard. So, I tried another tactic. I determined:
what needs to be replaced? My leggings were looking a little
weary, and some Sunday church slacks would be a wise
choice. Then, I ventured through the shoes. I noticed the
white and navy-blue New Balance like Dan always wore. I
winced at the ambush, then reasoning this: those are earthly
things. His soul has no use for these in Heaven. Thinking
of his joy in being with the Lord helped defuse the surge

that threatened to sweep me out to sea with a cascade of tears. In spite of myself, I smiled through those sudden tears because the boys always teased him for always buying the exact same pair of shoes! I felt like God provided that little spark of humor to stay by trembling knees and let me know: you can do this.

These little setbacks and victories are, in fact, ways I can redirect how I think about my ventures into shopping before I leave the house. This scripture promise says the Lord will hold my hand and that He reminds me not to fear, because He will help me through these tough situations. Like when our children first learn to cross the street, we teach them to hold our hand, we look both ways, and when it's safe, we cross the street. I guess some self-talk and prayer helps to manage our trips to places that may be triggers. Now, when I approach Home Depot or Lowes, I tell myself that it's safe here. I'm shopping for what's needed for my house. I know the Lord is holding my hand down these aisles. I look both ways, to the earthly reality and to the Heavenly reality. I know the Lord is helping me because it's become a bit easier.

These days of ambushes and triggers are likely to last awhile, if not always, on some level. But I can rely on the promise Jesus made to His followers about sending the Helper after He left for Heaven: "He will teach you all things and remind you all that I said to you." (John 14:26-27 NASB) The Comforter, Counselor, Helper will remind me of the promises I need to remember wherever I am, whatever I need, to recall what Jesus said: "My peace I give you...Do not let your heart be troubled."

Lord, Thank You for helping me venture out when I'd much rather stay hidden from triggers that might remind me of him, of our life together. You alone know how much I need Your strength for every step, every day. I surrender these triggers to You, and thank You for the grace to go shopping, the strength you give as I risk encountering sadness, knowing You are with me. In Jesus' Name, Amen

> **Grief notes: New experiences can be difficult as we begin to consider the one who is no longer with us. There may be more "losses" we realize as we step into this new territory. Shopping can bombard us with past experiences, products and places that remind us of our lives together, as well as seeing other couples that might remind us of our lives before loss. Shopping**

can also bring piped-in music, so there
may be songs that ambush us as we fill a
shopping cart.

"How happy (Blessed) is the one who does not walk in the advice of the wicked or stand in the pathway with sinners or sit in the company of mockers! Instead, his delight is in the Lord's instruction, and he meditates on it day and night." Psalm 1: 1-3

There are places where I don't shop for groceries. I don't take my shopping list to the convenience store, since I figure they don't have all the items I'd be looking for. I also don't shop where mostly near-expired goods are, as I am usually looking for fresher options. I usually don't go to the big bulk purchase stores, as I don't want to store items that might go stale before I can use them. So, I choose the store with the most options that are best for me. I think this can also apply to advice on how I feed my mind during grief. That means I'll be particular about what I read, watch, and listen to.

Psalm 1 truly sets the stage for making wise decisions about where to get advice. It clearly states that if we are seeking a life blessing, not to walk in the advice of the wicked, don't stand on the path of sinners, or sit around with those who are mockers. As I looked online at sites about widows, I was struck with how many dwelled on the never-ending sadness, the hopelessness of any future, that life had no more meaning. Rarely a mention of God, and sadly, seldom was there any reference to hope and eternal life. I realized that these sites had nothing to offer me. These were threads of advice that did not acknowledge the Lord, and in some cases, made a mockery of God. These weren't for me.

There are many podcasts and books offered online, but again, I used this as my gauge: "Instead, his delight is in the Lord's instruction, and he meditates on it day and night." I looked to see how God's Word was or was not used in writing about grief and loss. So many options might deal with grief with "the latest research", but if there was no scripture, no reference to our hope in Christ, I knew it would not help in my healing process nor would it give Godly guidance for my new journey as a widow. I wanted to read about Christian widows and how they dealt with grief. To read their stories and accounts of how the Holy Spirit brought comfort and guidance for their steps forward. Both Gayle Roper and Margaret Nyman had authored books that spoke of their faith journey as widows. I read and reread those books I found that fit the criteria of Christ-centered and brought hope as well as encouragement.

Yes, it is true: there's a blessing choosing reading materials and relationships that advance our faith, and reflect my value placed on God's Word in my life. For those I encounter who don't yet know the power of God's grace and hope in life, I am happy to share the experiences of how the Lord has brought hope and comfort like a beam of light in the darkest part of my life, and I could not do this without my Lord and Savior, Jesus.

Lord, I pray for wisdom as I seek out materials that would encourage me in this season. I want to keep your word at the center of my healing. May I share this hope I have in You with others who are struggling with grief without You. In Jesus' Name, Amen

> **Grief notes: Grief is mentally and emotionally tiring. Stressors take even more energy, sometimes more than we can handle, so we need to be aware of how we are feeling and slow down, pacing ourselves. Take the time to rest, to stay hydrated, and to eat something nutritious.**

Journal 15

"My flesh and my heart may fail, but God
is the strength of my heart and my portion
forever." Psalm 73:26

When all the newness around me reminds me of how
I miss the old days, it's a mix that is sure to bring triggers
that can sideline me. This start of a new month is Dan's
birthday month, a first without him. To make matters worse,
Central Texas weather has turned gray, drizzly, and cloudy.
Even sleep was disrupted with a three-hour thunderstorm
in the night that ushered out what was left of September.
Hello dreaded October. This will only be followed by holiday months that promise more triggers, more "firsts".

Gray. Everything seems gray: the day matches my mood.
And then, the gloom of this-is-how-it'll-always-be sets in:
Screeeech. Stop the tape right there. I'm realizing that this
is Enemy territory. Is that what the Enemy wants? Am I
sad because the weather changed? Am I feeling heart-heavy
because I'm heading toward Dan's first birthday in Heaven?

This weakness eats at me, weighs me down like a wet blanket. Hypersensitive. Yes, it is my flesh and my heart that seem to be failing. My flesh aches for what was; my heart remembers and can't quite believe this is a new normal.

It's true, my flesh and my heart are in ultimate weakness, needy, and floundering. It's also true that they may fail. Some days it seems possible. But God! God is the strength of my heart. He provides when I'm empty, depleted, and aching beyond words. He is Almighty, the God of Angel Armies, the rock of refuge. He energizes this heart with His eternal hope and promised presence, staying close to me. I can choose at this moment where I will go with trust. I can follow the spiraling path of sadness and despair, or I can choose to remember that God can be trusted always, as this season was His decision.

"And my portion forever" Yes, He is my inherited territory forever. Where I can abide, resting in Him. When I chose to trust Him for salvation, I was on the receiving end of His inheritance. Salvation, sins forgiven, the indwelling Holy Spirit, eternal life in Heaven, the position of a child of God, to name a few are now mine from the Father. It is all because of Jesus, my Portion. Step by step, I am learning to stake my tent here as I set out on this new journey. This is where I now dwell, abiding in this portion of His providence and protection. Thunderstorms and gray skies are subject to Him, but I will choose to remain and trust in His power, because I have only weakness. Heart and flesh failing? I know where my forever strength is. It is found in the Lord, alone. Forever.

Lord, these are hard days. The enemy is cruel with no pity for those sorrowing. He seeks only opportunities to kill, steal and destroy the weak. I also know this: Change is never easy, but You know me: my past, my present, and my future. You have seen all my life changes. I know I must choose to look to You and Your strength, to seek your grace for grief. You see my pain, and I pray You will bring purpose from it to serve You, for You are my eternal portion. In Jesus' Name, Amen

> **Grief notes: Grieving can make it seem like there is no light anywhere. But far above the clouds and pain, the sun is shining. Choosing to realize that there is hope above, we can see that our sadness is blocking out the light under this curtain of grief. So, I must take the time to face the grief before me, working through the loss, and see that God's hand is there to guide me back to purpose and light.**

Journal 16

"Lord, hear my prayer; let my cry for help
come before You. Do not hide your face
from me in my day of trouble. Listen closely
to me; answer me quickly when I call."
Psalm 102: 1-2

This Psalm was one of many that became my prayer, my
cry for help in the early days of trouble. How quickly I wanted
His answers when I called out to Him!

In the middle of grief, I'm finding myself asking questions: what is next going forward? What am I to do with my
time, with all my household belongings stacked in storage,
with family here and there? Where's my place and what's my
role now that it's just me? The frayed ends keep unraveling
it seems. Where shall I live? Some days I feel at loose ends
while an urgency to find an answer gnaws at me. Patience, I
remind myself. Take some time. Seek wisdom. Everyone says
wait a year before making a major change. Times like this are

when I need Dan to help me peer through this fog, but, yes, it's only me now.

So, I'm beginning to some read books written by Christian widows who have traveled this path and am encountering some good advice. Without a doubt, they all recommend taking time before any big decisions, taking time to grieve, and working through grief, as well as seeking God's leading and guidance. This sounds like wisdom. And it sounds like waiting with patience.

Thankfully the local church I attend has a grief group, and that gives a regular time to talk and process a lot about what happens in grief, what to expect, what triggers emotions, and to hear others' stories of loss. I can identify with their pain as they recount struggles with realizing their loved one is gone.

All things take time, so step by step, I'm gaining some confidence on unsteady legs. I'm learning to navigate this new city and finding courage not to stay in my room all day. The Lord's constant help with loads of grace for these pain-filled days has given me hope, a reliable hope because His help has been available and real. His comfort is real. His peace and strength have been genuinely present. Because of all He has done, I know He will be just as faithful in the details of this life in transition where I so miss Dan. I know the Lord hears my prayers, and I know He will answer with just what I need. Yes, in His time, He will lead me where He intends for me to go, what He has planned for me to do, and how I will serve Him on this new journey.

Lord, You are my help, my steady comforter and I can rely on answers when I call to You. Your compassionate mercies are new every morning, so great is Your faithfulness. Every morning when I awake to realize that this is my new reality, Your grace covers me. I am trusting You for answers to dilemmas and fears that will arise, so I won't borrow worries for the "what ifs" of tomorrow. Thank You for the hope and strength that are mine all because of Your sufficient grace. In Jesus' Name, Amen

Grief notes: The first year of grief is full of "firsts". The first holidays, anniversaries, birthdays, special significant days since our beloved passed can be difficult days. Anticipating them with a plan in mind can help alleviate the triggering of emotions beyond what is already a time full of memories. Sometimes it seems anticipating the day is more wrought with emotions than the actual day.

Journal 17

"How long will I store up anxious concerns
within me, agony in my mind every day?"
Psalm 13:2

List in hand, walking through the grocery store and
suddenly, I am ambushed by a song! I could feel the sob
start deep in my chest, and I hurried through the rest of
the shopping. Hot tears were falling as I pushed my cart
toward the car. How long will grief be this raw? I was feeling
stronger! And now, all over again, I am dissolving into a
doubt of my progress.

How long indeed. When a song can bring up a memory
of a tender moment, the waves of grief hit hard like an
undertow carrying me out past my ability to get ahead of
that thought. In moments of ambush and sadness, it's like
the Enemy whispers that this will never end. Any hope of
joy is out of the picture. It's all about love and grief, right?
The two things that change us is that as deeply as we loved,
we will grieve as deeply. For a lifetime love, there is only

giving it to the Lord for guidance down this path of acceptance and the journey toward new purpose in a new season.

Then I read Psalm 25: 4-6, "Make your ways known to Me, Lord; teach me Your paths. Guide me in Your truth and teach me, for You are the God of my salvation; I wait for You all day long. Remember, Lord, Your compassion and Your faithful love for they have existed since antiquity." That is a long time, a long track record of faithful love. This season, this transition is the start of a new work in me. How long will this take? That, too, is in His hands. His compassionate, faithful love is from eternity to eternity. I trust that He will be there, teaching me the way because He is the Way, guiding me with His truth since He is the Truth, and He is The Life. Maybe this isn't the life I had in mind, but this Life is the one He designed, allowed, and purposed for me.

Anxious concerns and agony of mind are companions in grief, but as David says in Psalm 27:13-14, "I am certain that I will see the Lord's goodness in the land of the living. Wait for the Lord, be strong, and let your heart be courageous. Wait for the Lord." He has blessed me, comforted me, and given peace at every asking, so why would this time be different? I will wait for what He has in store for me.

So, I will give to Him these waves that hit me, randomly. Ambushes. I know that in the waiting, He is here beside me giving me the strength and peace like no other to overcome the wave and bring me back to shore. How long will ambushes and triggers continue to happen? I don't know. What I do know is God has a long history of faithful love. I can trust His presence in the surprise swells and mighty wave for He is good at calming the storms.

Lord, sometimes this grieving grabs me, ambushes me and I weep deeply. But I'm learning to wait for Your compassion to comfort me, Your long-standing faithful love to bring peace. Thank You for Your presence, Holy Comforter, Eternal Counselor. You often intervene with mercy in this pain. But I'm learning that tears are healing, so I praise You for that, too. In Jesus' Name, Amen

> **Grief notes: During grief, there are two ways of being alone. One is isolation where we withdraw from everyone and reject all interactions with everyone. The other is solitude, when we realize we need alone time to sort through emotions, weep, pray and read the Bible. Isolation can lead to complications in grief, but solitude can be a healing step in sorting out our new lives and finding needed strength.**

Journal 18

"The angel of the Lord encamps around
those who fear Him and rescues them."
Psalm 34:7

Rescue. I have a childhood memory of a rescue at
Yosemite National Park in California. Our family awaited
the nightly Firefall where glowing embers were poured
from the top of Glacier Point 3,000 feet to the valley floor
beneath. (Yes, this was before 1968 when the nearly100 year
Firefall tradition was stopped.) As we waited for the falling
fire to light up the night sky, there came a message through
the crowd that a hiker, who'd taken what he thought was a
shortcut, was stranded on a one-foot ledge 600 feet above
us. It was dark, and bullhorns kept the teen awake all night
until morning when rangers rappelled within 100 feet and
threw a rope to the young man who'd spent the night on
one foot. In my head, I can still hear those bullhorns, "We
are on the ledge above you. Stay awake. Do not move." As in
grief, I can now see how often in these past weeks the voice
of God's Word has reminded me of His nearness, keeping

me calmed and comforting me. Rescuing me from despair, helping me see in the darkest of nights that I can trust Him and His promises of rescue.

In this season, I know the Lord is near me. I'm reminded daily how much I am relying on His nearness. His peace settles my ragged nerves and sorrowing thoughts as well as providing the hope that gives me strength, that strength I need to wait on His directing me. These reassurances all come from His encamping presence. When the incoming tide of emotion threatens to sink me, I turn my thoughts to realize this: He is near. And no, I am not alone. I hear His voice in His Word reminding me: I am here, stay in My comfort. Abide in Me.

"I will never leave you nor forsake you" How often I have leaned on that promise since Dan passed. When the waves of memory roll over me and tears come, I recall these words and fix my thoughts on how close God is and His faithfulness to rescue me when I feel helpless and in need of direction. When memories ache, I know that He is my way through this valley. Even before, He had been my source of rescue in countless ways, even more so now as I start this new journey of being a widow. I am not alone, for the angel of the Lord is encamping around me, ready to help. He is above me; He alone knows this ledge and this dark night.

He will not only rescue me, but He will safely put me on His intentional path of purpose and service.

Lord, I am so thankful for Your presence and being there when I need You most. You know my needs before I even ask. You encamp so close, I know You are near me now. Your Holy Spirit's comfort is always complete and timely. I pray You will lead me to share with others the gospel story so they, too, can be assured of this encamping comfort as well as the peace and rescue that comes only from You. In Jesus' Name, Amen

Grief note: In grief, we all need comforting. How we find comfort is important to the health of our grieving. If we turn to unhealthy practices to numb the pain of loss, we are at risk of debt, addiction, or disease that would complicate our healing. Spending time with a new hobby, painting, or exercising can be a source of help on our new path, giving us a new way to grow.

Journal 19

"This is my comfort in my affliction: Your promise has given me life." Psalm 119: 50

I am no longer Dan's wife, and this is a huge role-change for me and a significant identity loss. So, who am I now? Our children and grandchildren stand in testimony that together we raised some great kids! I see so much in them that reflects their Dad and Grandpa. I also see answered prayers and promises kept. As many widows do, I ask myself about those promises that have given me life. These many promises of who I am in Christ give me comfort and an identity.

I am **forgiven**! Ephesians 1:7 says I am forgiven, redeemed. Because Christ purchased me, I look to Him for how I can now serve Him best.

Deuteronomy 7:6 says I am His **treasured possession**. He redeemed us! His Son's blood redeemed us from the curse of sin and death. Verse 9 says, "Know that the Lord your God is God, the faithful God Who keeps His gracious covenant loyalty for a thousand generations with those who love Him and keep His commands." He is a faithful keeping God!

Acts 17:28 says I am **God's child**. We can come to God the Father because of our inheritance through Jesus' work on the cross and the indwelling Holy Spirit, we can call Him "Abba" Father. A father always knows what their child needs, especially our Creator Father. He made me, designed me, and knows my life path.

Colossians 3:12 says I'm **chosen, holy, and dearly loved**. Yes, before the world began, He knew me, and He designed the purpose for my life. Psalm 57:2 says, "I cry out to God Most High, to God who fulfills His purpose for me."

Philippians 3:20 says I am a **citizen of Heaven**. Philippians 4:1 says, "Therefore (So, consequently) stand firm in the Lord!" Yes, even though life looks so different, this transition seems so hard, and now is not the time to quit trusting His plan!

Philippians 4:13 says that through Him Who strengthens me, **I am able to do all things**.

And 2 Timothy 1:7 reminds me **I'm empowered by Him**. He has given me the Spirit of power, love, and sound judgment.

It's true: God's Word has many precious promises which gives me hope and peace. Who I am in Him gives me comfort and assurance for the journey ahead. God's Word will guide me through this season, for His promises are giving me life.

Lord, I'm thankful for all Your Word assures me of. I am learning of all that I am and have in You, and now that is what I cling to. When You say I am complete, strengthened by Your might, lacking nothing, I know it is true. In Jesus' Name, Amen

> **Grief notes: Grief can make time seem strange. Sometimes it seems it was all just yesterday, and yet at the same moment it can seem like it was years ago. We look at the passing of time since we were married, and we think "How can it be that long? It's like yesterday!" It seems time is elastic. It's all part of the brain in grief. Someone suggested writing an overview of decades to help with putting it all together.**

Journal 20

"As citizens of Heaven, live your life worthy of the Gospel of Christ." Philippians 1:27 (CSB)

A citizen of Heaven. Now that's an identity to ponder! Dan is now a citizen in residence, in the very presence of God. I, too, am a citizen of Heaven, but still in foreign residence. My dear husband is free of the tethers of grief, sadness, entanglements and distractions of a sin-broken world. Yet, I am here, subject to the sorrow of separation, the tears of loss and sadness, but my citizenship offers: hope, peace, assurance. One day through the hope of salvation, we will see each other again, not in our earthly roles, but better. That brings a measure of peace when I let that soak down into my soul. Real peace. The surpassing-understanding kind. The assurance we have in Christ, because of the Cross, and the Resurrection brings living hope as promises from God, who cannot lie.

Yes, my future is in a heavenly home, mansions built and prepared by our Lord. For this I am compelled and drawn by love to live worthy of Christ's gospel, taking every opportunity to share that good news with others. This new pathway means I must look up from the pain of loss and realize what a treasure I have in Christ, knowing that this comfort, peace, and hope is what others need to know, too. I shudder when I think of going through this pain and sorrow without the Lord. Living my life worthy of the Gospel of Christ also makes me aware that I am an ambassador for Him, with an urgency that others may find Him. We live in a world loved by God in such a way that He sent Jesus to provide eternal life and hope, yet so many are filling their sad souls with worthless substitutes for His hope and grace.

As I continue along this journey the Lord has called me to, I trust Him for grace to handle what hurts, strength when the weakness of grief hits hard, and wisdom for the next steps. His faithful gracious promises are the currency I depend on to live this life worthy of the One Who bought my salvation, and they keep me moving forward. Yes, I am a citizen of Heaven living for the Lord, relying on His wisdom for entrusting me with this journey. I know there's still a purpose for me here, so I lean in and double down on trust-and-obey decisions. Besides, reaching out to share the Lord Jesus Christ with someone who doesn't know Him helps me remember why I am still here.

Lord, Thank You for the hope I have in You that even now I can live with the perspective of a Citizen of Heaven where Jesus is seated at the right hand of the Majesty on High, making intercession for us! One day I will be a citizen in residence, like my beloved is, but until that day, I will make use of my time and opportunities to help others find Your gospel, receive the gift of salvation, so that they, too, may become citizens of Heaven, Your kingdom. In Jesus' Name, Amen.

> **Grief notes: This time of grief can be like a tangled ball of yarn. The minute we feel some acceptance, then we can be right back to tears and wondering why. We might catch ourselves laughing, then suddenly feel overcome guilt for finding something humorous. Just know there's no set way to grieve, no set time. We are all unique, so find some comfort that some days will be sunnier, some will be**

stormy, and we will continue to heal if we are nurturing our soul and spirit by drawing close to God.

Journal 21

"When I am filled with cares, Your comfort
brings me joy." Psalm 94:19

Filled with cares. Additional Bible versions might say
"great anxiety within me, doubts, a multitude of thoughts".
In other words, when I am troubled, His comfort makes
me glad, soothes my soul, delights, and gives me reason to
continue walking forward on this day. Sitting with this verse
as well as 2 Corinthians 1:3-4, the Father of mercies, the
God of all comfort has definitely been filling this heart like
nothing else, leaving little room for the cares, anxieties, and
doubts that try their best to take up real estate in my soul.

I know those moments still hit me just when I think I
am a little stronger. There will be an unexpected memory,
a phrase, a place will cross my thinking and my sorrow
crushes in on me, hitting my chest with a wallop that only
grieving the loss of my beloved can do. And I realize all over
again: I am a widow. A solo life ahead, as far as I can see:
no private conversations, no shared adventures. It's just me.
No joy. Cue the pity party music.

No! The Lord's promise is that He will never leave me nor forsake me. He's been with me for 49 years! He was with us! He is my Light, Bread of Life, Good Shepherd, The Door, the Way, the Truth and the Life. Besides all of those roles, He is the Joy that is my strength! Strength! Like Nehemiah telling the Israelites not to be dejected and sad when they heard the Word of God and how they had disappointed the Lord. This was a holy time to remember and celebrate all God had done "because they understood the words that were explained to them." (v. 12) That joy was a source of strength! What a great reminder that the joy of the Lord is the power we need, and no changeable emotion compares to that deep knowing who we are in Him.

Yes, when I'm filled with the cares of being a widow, God's comfort brings relief and because I trust that He is for me, I know that He ordained and allowed this new course of life for me. Through the fruit of His Spirit, joy will blossom. Joy is seated deep within me, fed with the promises of His Word and the assurance of faith. It is the Living Hope I have through the Lord Jesus Christ, so I can choose His Joy even when I don't feel like it. 1 Peter 1:8 says, "You love Him, though you have not seen Him. And though not seeing Him now, you believe in Him and rejoice with inexpressible and glorious joy."

I believe in Him and all He has done and is doing. I can choose His Joy because He, the Father of mercies and God of all comfort, surrounds me with the promises that brings me peace that passes understanding. He gives light for the way, and grace for the moments that still ambush me. And yet He delights to bring me that Joy, inexpressible and glorious joy.

Lord, Thank You for Your gracious comfort and joy. You are the God of all comfort, giving me strength for whatever I'm called to do. I trust You, Lord, and thank You for reminding me that I can cast all these cares and stressors onto You. I want to step with assurance along this path, so I'm leaning on You to be the Lamp for the way You've put before me. In Jesus' Name, Amen.

> **Grief notes: Our bodies take time to catch up with our grief. It takes a half a year or more for our hearts to comprehend what our brain knows. That's why we often wake up in the morning and tell ourselves all over again: He is no longer here. Or we awaken in the night, only to remind ourselves he is gone. In time, acceptance comes.**

Journal 22

"Trust in Him at all times you people; pour out your hearts before Him. God is our refuge." Psalm 62:8

At all times, trust in Him. In grieving, some of those times, some days are harder than others and more likely to bring memory ambushes. Dan's first "heavenly" birthday is this week. I must remember this: he has moved to Heaven and is with Jesus Himself. He's with the One Who so loved us, that He gave the World the best gift ever: eternal life through His Son's sacrifice. Because of His great love and His great promises to be with me and never forsake me, I know I can have faith in Him. I make the choice to trust that He will direct my faltering feet, and that He will give me hope and a future. It means I can have confidence in all He is doing to guide every step forward.

Trust Him. Really trust Him for strength. Rely on Him when the waves of aloneness-realization hits. It means throwing all my weak-knee, gut-punch, breath-stealing reactions onto His immense riches-of-glory shoulders. Really trusting Him for wisdom every day when there are car titles, bank accounts, and insurance companies to change, taxes to organize, not to mention all the what's-next questions. It means really having faith in Him for the grace I need to manage my thinking, communicating, and reactions to this new pathway. When saying "Me", where for 42 years I'd said "We", I need His grace. Like an all-weather, steel-belted radial on this journey, creating a cushion between this new life, and the jolts of reality, grace is giving me courage for the road ahead.

So, I pour out my heart to Him. What do I need? Sometimes, it's just "Help, Lord" or "Oh, Lord." He knows what we ask before we even speak, spirit-groans interpreted by the Holy Spirit. And He moves in with Peace and a calm reminder of His presence. Those anniversaries, birthdays, evenings, long, sagging weekends that seem unending. The Lord is there. When I'm pining over the memories of Dan, his sense of adventure, his MacGyver-like engineering creativity, his take-charge motivation, the layers of loss carve away at my heart, and the Lord pours comfort into those echoing caverns.

Yes, God is my refuge, that safe place bringing reassurance and peace in the storm. Recognizing times and places where ambushes may likely happen, I ask in advance for support. Like holidays and special days. Before feelings and emotions can batter my day, I pray a Psalm or I read verses of hope and provision, then I pray for the strength I need for the tasks ahead. I try to remind myself to be thankful that Dan was prepared for this move to Heaven, and I am truly grateful that this separation is just temporary. Heaven awaits. I recall this: God has promised His presence here with me, so I can walk on in His strength, His wisdom, and His grace. What a blessing to have an eternal living hope in Christ and know there is no safer refuge.

Lord, I am so thankful I can always trust You and pour out my needs to You. Every detail. I am grateful that You are my refuge, my place of safety in the storms of grief. My "house" is built on this strong Rock of safety, so I can run to You, I can trust in You. In Jesus' Name, Amen

> **Grief notes: Grief is not a fifty-yard dash. It takes time, so invest in doing the work of grief. Tears are healing, so weep when you must. Don't let anyone make you feel as if your grief is going on too long. Every heart grieves differently, it seems, and**

those who would rush you, simply give them grace and walk on knowing your healing will come as you work on your own journey.

Journal 23

"When Jesus spoke again to the people, He said, "I am the Light of the world. Whoever follows Me will never walk in darkness but will have the light of life." John 8:12

"Let you light shine before others, that they may see your good deeds and glorify your Father in Heaven." Matthew 5:16

The night Dan passed, I felt like a light in me went out. Dimness took over, and it was like I had half the light. But I remember that Jesus said He is the Light of the World and whoever follows Him won't walk in darkness. I follow Him, so why allow the dark? I did not need to continue walking in the half-light dimness, I reasoned, because the Light of Life, Jesus, abides within me. I reminded myself of this: Dan is in Heaven, bathed in God's glorious light, present with the Lord, and that began to give me peace. It's the same peace I experience knowing that God Himself is with me in this time, bringing me through the daily ups and downs with His strength and comfort.

The Lord Jesus said, "Let your light shine," so what good I do for Christ, will glorify my Father in Heaven. It's becoming a new way to think about life in this painful place that is so easily dark: sharing the light. When someone asks how I'm doing, I can reply, "I'm doing as good as can be expected, but the Lord has been such a Help and comfort to me!" Knowing that not one step of this journey is a surprise to God, I can turn to Him for wisdom and the grace He knew I'd need at this point. He gives me grace to awaken to the light each day and to remind myself: this is where I am. I need that grace to still my waking mind in the middle of the night: yes, it's true. Dan's no longer here. In the dark, I remind myself of John 1: 4, "In Him was life, and that life was the Light of men." The very Source of Light and radiance for mankind. Amazing? Yes, amazing. He is the Light of my comfort and peace.

My earthly light may dim with loss, but as I step out into the light of Jesus, I continue to call on Him for His light to shine on my uncertain steps. His light of reassurance shines upon my way so I'll need never stumble in dimness, or fear for my footing. As I share with others all the ways He met me with hope, I can reflect that Light for others.

Lord, I am thankful that You are the Light of the world. Whenever I feel the dimness of loss creeping in, a shadow over my aching heart, may I turn to face you, honestly telling You of my pain, fears, and sadness. You know this already, but I bring it all into Your pure light of Truth: Your sovereign perspective. I want to reflect You in every step, every action shining with Your grace, directing me forward when I cannot do it on my own power. Only in You, Lord, can I find the way to walk through this grief to healing and purpose. In Jesus' Name, Amen

Grief notes: Sometimes, folks just don't know what to say to those who have lost a loved one. They usually speak with the best intentions, but at times it comes across awkwardly. A simple "How are you?" suddenly becomes just as awkward to answer. "Fine" is not the answer you want to give because in all reality, you are not "Fine". You might say, "As good as can be expected" or "Every day is a little different, but God has been so good". Unless you are in a situation where they

are going to sit with you and listen to what your life is like now, a shorter answer that gives an honest reply is sufficient.

"For it is God who is working in you both to will and to work according to His good purpose." Philippians 2:13

It had been our plan after selling our Oregon home to move to Texas, buy a house, and get all new furniture. We'd spent the better part of a year redoing our home, downsizing, three dumpsters-full gone, many trips to donate what we'd deemed no longer necessary. I'd willingly relinquished the old stuff, knowing new things, a new start lay ahead. Oh, my and did it.

Then Covid hit us, and suddenly Dan was gone. Next came gut-wrenching, heart-rending grief. So, with his passing, all hope of that new place, new furniture would all become unrealized dreams. So much for the new start. A door had shut, and this began an entirely new unanticipated season. A new path where I would be learning to rely on the Lord.

Fast forward a few months, and I'm out furniture shopping with my sister who'd also relocated to Central Texas.

She turns to me saying, "What do you think of this chair?" How can I help someone else pick out their living room set? This wasn't supposed to be this way. I begin to feel the sharp pain of a newly realized loss.

Stop. This is God's way and it was His plan. He understands the toll of loss. I am realizing that Dan's passing has a higher purpose. So, I began to see it. It's not about my giving up what we had anticipated together. It is about learning to navigate a completely new life. A new plan, a new view of life. It's God's purpose in the pain transcending any new house, furniture, or more "stuff" of this world. It's looking at His eternal reasons for this loss and how I am learning how to walk without collapsing and giving in to the Enemy's fear. This is so much bigger. This far outweighs any earthly "move" Dan and I might have been planning. I wait now to see: what other purposes will be revealed in time, in the months and years ahead? What will the eternal fallout be of one life being taken? Like a pebble tossed onto a lake, the rings and ripples will range far and wide, these effects of his passing. All the more reason to recommit daily to His guidance and seek His face in it all.

So, it's dawning on me how God had dislocated my sense of value and importance. This new view of priorities is a paradigm shift. He's working in me what is foremost to Him. And I'm thinking that it's a gift. It's His work moving me along to what His plan is willing and working of His good purpose that is unique to me from this place of pain and loss that makes me see life differently now. Choosing to trust each step, I know He is moving me and changing what I deem important. Willing and working. Always. Just as His purpose will always be done, He is working a change in me.

Lord, I confess that some days I've looked about and noticed what I'm missing, how I wanted life to turn out. But now, I can see that You are working in me, changing me to truly make Your will a priority. I surrender all this transition to You and Your ways of grace knowing You will make it all work for the good in Your timing, not mine. In Jesus' Name, Amen.

> **Grief notes: Dealing with our loved one's belongings can be difficult. Go through their things only when you are ready. There is no rush. In time, you can pass on items to your children, grandchildren, and relatives, but do it in your time frame. It is hard but it's also part of your healing to go through their things.**

Journal 25

"Those who know Your name trust in You because You have not abandoned those who seek, You, Lord." Psalm 9:10

We value our names and try to carry them wisely. Our reputations are at stake! God's name is known to David here as one who could be trusted and would not abandon him. What a blessing to understand that we can wholeheartedly trust the Lord to be present in our need.

More than anything, I'm realizing how the Lord has been sustaining me, how strong His grace is during intense grief. How have I survived? I can now see how He has provided peace moment by moment in the swells of sadness. He's been there with me in the late evenings when I didn't want to fall asleep and possibly dream that Dan is here, then awake with disappointment and renewed shock.

I know now, more than ever, what God can do in the furnace of grief. I know I can call on His name for strength when weakness would keep me immobilized. I know I can pray and He will bring peace when the storm and the waves of anxiety are relentless. When fear stretches as far as my heart can see, I can call on His name and His grace enfolds me. His word has fed me what I need to continue. I can trust at a new level I've never known, never had to experience before, but He is there.

"Those who know Your name trust in You." Suddenly I'm reminded how many don't know His name, to call on Him, to have the support of trusting, and knowing His love. Even in a season of grief and suffering, I can see I am blessed. I understand this: God's comfort is real. I need to share this hope with others whose tears fall on solitary pillows.

Lord, I am so thankful that both of us walked with You, knew Your name, and trusted in You. We were seeking You together for Your will, Your direction, as well as praying for our sons and their families to walk with You. Not once did You abandon us. I know Your Holy Plan meant he would be called Home to Heaven before me, so I trust You left me here for a special reason. I know You have not forsaken me here, because Your sufficient grace will lead me on to the role You have for me in this new season. In Jesus' Name, Amen

Grief notes: Journaling is such a great opportunity to process our feelings, emotions, and put into words what our needs or concerns are. It's also a wonderful way to write about the verses that bring healing to our broken hearts and light to our way. Over the course of time, we can see how our journey is moving forward and all the ways God is working in our lives.

Journal 26

"The heart knows its own bitterness, and no
outsider shares its joy… Even in laughter a
heart may be sad, and joy may end in grief."
Proverbs 14: 10, 13

How vividly the sharp pain of loss has been brought
home to me. Losing Dan makes me wonder, will I ever
really laugh again? I'll momentarily chuckle at something,
and I feel guilty. How can I laugh? My heart feels that is so
alien. All the years of joyful memories and suddenly here
I am, I'm reviewing them all, it seems. No one else could
really share in them nor know them. My whole being aches
with that thought. It's true that only the heart knows its
capacity for love and loss.

Then I recall the words of Jesus: "Peace I leave with
you, My peace I give you. I do not give you as the world
gives. Do not let your hearts be troubled and do not be
afraid." (John 14:27) Psalm 94:19 says, "When I am filled
with cares, Your comfort brings me joy." Considering that

loss can bring bitterness, or that, on the other hand, I can have joy because of the eternal source of peace in the Lord, I realize it is the Holy Spirit working within me. He's no outsider. He has shared in every moment all the years of our married lives! In every memory, the Lord was there. He knows and carries them with me! That alone helps my heart turn a corner.

Yes, even in a moment I may laugh, yet there is still sadness, like a shade on my heart. And even with joy, the reassured knowing of all the blessings the Lord has provided, there is still grief. The grief is there because I love. And I miss him. I miss us. My heart knows. But I also know peace. The not-like-the-world-gives peace. His peace that He's left with me by the inner dwelling of the Holy Spirit, reminding me that joy is still possible. Healing is possible. New purpose is possible. Meanwhile, He is helping me carry the memories, holding my guilt while I laugh, and although my joy right now might end with grief later, there still is joy.

As the layers of grief surface from the fog of my widow's path, I know that He will bring healing, guidance, hope. And joy. In it all, my heart knows and trusts, even though the process of grief is not a straight line. It ebbs and flows and realizes new losses from time to time, and I again experience the pangs that catch me in an ambush. But I am learning to stop, remember that His ways are higher, there is an eternal plan, and He is with me, never to abandon me. These are the reassuring components of my enduring joy.

Lord, I'm realizing in my grief, the depth of love and loss that my heart recognizes from the bitter sadness to the memories You help me to carry. May I recall that You understand my pain and will provide the comfort, peace, and strength I need, for You see what I need before I even ask. I am ever so thankful for Your presence and the promise of joy. In Jesus' Name, Amen

> **Grief notes: Turning on praise and worship music can help change a sad moment or a sad day. Uplifting songs can help redirect our hearts and minds to the One who asks us to cast all our cares on Him. It can turn our hearts to gratitude for blessings He gave to you and your beloved as well as thankfulness for the years God gave you together.**

Journal 27

"Happy is the person whose strength is in You, whose hearts are set on pilgrimage…As they pass through the Valley of Baca (tears), they make it a source of spring water; even the autumn rains will cover it in blessings. They go from strength to strength; each appears before God in Zion." Psalm 84:5-7

As I understand it, a pilgrimage is a long journey, a quest, a mission to a holy place usually for spiritual growth. In many ways, this grief journey seems like a pilgrimage. I'm discovering along the way how closely I need to walk with the Lord, to know the promises in His Word, and to ask for and rely on His strength, as well as stay in prayer. The psalmist says the happy person has their heart set on pilgrimage. Being set means being determined. Being intentional. Fixed. Purposeful. Can I say that about this widow's journey I'm on? Am I determined to see God's sovereign hand and plan? Am I intentional about my reading, journaling, and prayer? Am I staying fixed on Him as my source of help, strength, and peace? Am I being purposeful by seeking His purposes and goals for this new season in life?

While passing through this Valley of Tears, the pilgrim is making this area a source of fresh water for their soul. This valley can be a challenge, and sometimes I think I'm out of the deep parts, but no. I am in the Valley of Tears yet again. Am I aware of the autumn rain blessings I'm receiving? Am I recognizing the blessing of new friendships, or moping about wishing for what used to be? And then there's my stamina. Some things I just don't have the "bandwidth" for right now. Political talk is one. Gossip. Bickering. Some things no longer hold my interest and tend to just make me anxious. What I now value in life has changed. My heart and purpose have been dislocated. I am finding new eternal priorities. Yes, sometimes I still feel I am going from strength to strength, trying to pay attention to my rest level and how stressors affect my "full cup" of emotions. Do I pay attention to my nutrition? Not eating, lack of rest, and exposure to added tension all play havoc with my strength. Something to remember—grief takes energy.

Psalm 139: 1-5 reminds me that along this route, God searches us, knows when I sit down and when I stand up; He understands my thoughts from far away, observing my travels and my rest. He is aware of all my ways, having encircled me and placed His hand upon me. Not even darkness can hide me from His eye, for verse 12 says, "The night shines like the day; darkness and light are alike to You." This is a happy reassurance on this pilgrimage that His faithful love and presence is with me!

Yes, each of these "happy ones" on pilgrimage appears before God in Zion. I'm encouraged that He is so fully aware of all my moments, the ups and downs, and the valleys. He sees my progress toward healing and what's most important to me now. He sees the setbacks and the rugged ways. "He knows the path I take…" (Job 23:10). And He will see that I make it to the mountain top.

Lord, You see me. You see me in the Valley of Tears and all along this widow's journey pilgrimage. You also see and prepare me for what lies ahead of me. You bring blessings I could not foresee, the provisions of friendship, community, and fellowship and for those I am truly thankful. In Jesus' Name, Amen

> **Grief notes: Be kind to yourself. You alone know the amount of energy it takes for moving forward hour by hour, day by day. Take each step knowing you are gaining strength.**

Journal 28

"Your word is a lamp for my feet and a light on my path." Psalms 119:105

The lamp of a lighthouse serves a variety of purposes along a waterway to help boats make safe passage in dangerous areas. Whether its sweeping light reveals shallows or hazardous rocky shorelines, it also shines to guide travelers into harbors. Lately I've been realizing that God's Word is such a guide for this journey, warning me of dangers, showing me how to proceed, and helping me find safe harbor.

"And now what shall I do?" Being a wife brought a lot of structure and order to my life. But that all changed when Dan passed into Heaven and I became a "Widow". As I now go along the path of this widow's journey, I wonder: what is ahead? I search the promises of God. It's one step at a time that the light spills just before me, lighting my feet, one step at a time. I'm relieved that this seems to be God's gracious way, in His wisdom, to reveal a bit of the route at a time. I would have been so fearful if I'd have known beforehand all that these last months have held of loss, grief, and heartache. That it would be "me", not "us" walking this route. But it's a different future now. Little did I know how precious and vital His Word and promises would become, a real lifeline for me in the dark. This lamp of His word and the light shows how I can navigate going forward.

God's eternal comfort and peace are so real to me now and there is a new depth of trusting. His sovereignty has reinforced my absolute deep trust in His ways and thoughts being so much higher than mine. His light, dispelling the dim uncertainty, shows me that I can rely on His wisdom when I ask for help. The lamp of His scripture reminds me I can be strengthened with power in my inner being (Ephesians 3:14-16); He will take care of all my needs (Philippians 4:19); I can come to Him for rest (Matthew 11: 28-30); He won't abandon me (Joshua 1:5); and I have a promise that nothing can separate me from the love of God (Romans 8:38).

His Word has been a guiding light for this trek so far. In fact, like a lantern on a dark night, the light shines right before each footfall, so I'll take this journey, trusting as I step. With His light leading my way onward, I have confidence in Him to find safe harbor, hope, peace, and the purpose He's prepared for me. He is with me, won't abandon me, and He's already gone before me, so He knows what lies ahead.

Lord, I praise You for Your inimitable wisdom, mercy, comfort, and guiding. You light the steps You have purposed for me. They will be revealed in Your time, in Your Holy plan. I know you will prepare me, sustain me, and give me grace along the way for every need. I lean on Your faithful presence for the days when the enemy will try to distract and side-track me along this path You have called me to. In Jesus' Name, Amen

> **Grief notes: Take note of how you have grown over the weeks and months of grief. You are taking on and learning how to do more tasks because you must. You are making decisions you may have never made before. You might be surprised to find that you are becoming stronger in new ways.**

Journal 29

"Rejoice in hope, be patient in affliction, be
persistent in prayer." Romans 12:12

Daily reaching for the Word as I wake up has been
part of my lifeline and so is prayer. Prayer, like "I need You
today, Lord…I need Your comfort…You promise that those
who mourn will be comforted. You promise that those who
wait on You will renew their strength. Today I will need
Your strength…" His promises give me hope that He hears
and answers my prayers.

Hope. I am mining the scriptures for hope daily, for that
is where I can start the first feeble widow-steps of rejoicing.
As I count my blessings, I rejoice that Dan knew Christ as
Savior. I rejoice that our sons know the Lord. I rejoice that
my grandkids love to hear about and sing about Jesus. I
rejoice that Heaven is, and one day there will be together-
ness again with Christ.

Patient in affliction: Ooooh, this is hard work, this grief.
Sometimes I want to rush it, step ahead of the pain, and
sidestep the sadness. But that doesn't work, does it? It stacks

up like traffic on the Interstate at rush hour. It reminds me of the kids singing "We're Going on a Lion Hunt": "Can't go over it, can't go under it, can't go around it, you have to go through it!" So, through it I go. I face the fear because I know the Enemy behind it, I accept the reminders of loss, and mentally recite the scriptures that strengthen my ankles to climb and to walk. I know only time and God's grace will walk me through this Valley, but the Word and prayer are the sustaining factors in the waves and storms of grieving.

Staying persistent in prayer is critical. Constant communication with Jesus is so important. I'm calling on the Lord for needs, for comfort, for help, guidance, direction, and wisdom. I know where my help and strength come from: the Lord because He is the Maker, Sustainer, Upholder of all things by the Word of His power. Colossians 4:2 says to devote ourselves to, persevere in, prayer; stay alert in it with thanksgiving. So, staying faithful on this course, I will keep short, frequent conversations with God: Praise You, Thank You, "How do I do this, Lord?", "Show me the way!", and my most-used: "Help, Lord!" Persistently. Consistently. Keeping that conversation going not only gives me someone to process life with, but it's a reminder that He is ever-present and ready to assist me in all my needs.

Philippians 4 says, "Rejoice always." That rejoicing lives in the gladness Christ brings and all He has done, the complete protection of God's unfathomable peace even in affliction. It's not worrying but submitting everything to Him through prayer. Persistent prayer. And that makes me rejoice in His eternal hope.

Lord, I'm thankful I know where hope comes from so I can rejoice in Your faithfulness. I'm grateful You hear my persistent prayers for comfort, help, and grace for this new way of life. As You were with Job, You knew how it would turn out for him, You are the same for me. Teach me to listen, to hear, and follow You as I hope in You, wait patiently for your guidance, and continue to persistently pray. In Jesus' Name, Amen

> **Grief notes: One of the biggest losses for widows is someone to process life with. We miss having someone who listens to us as we sort out everyday happenings. It was someone who offered their views, helped brainstorm, and problem solve. We begin to realize how valuable our prayer life can be when we start turning these over to God in our conversations with Him.**

Journal 30

"Do not fear, for I am with you; do not be afraid, for I am your God; I will strengthen you; I will help you; I will hold on to you with My righteous right hand." Isaiah 41:10

There is more than enough fear in the world today. Fear of disease, fear of what the future holds, fear of losing money on a deal, fear of failure, fear of someone or something that might hurt you, and of course, the fear of death. For the child of God, His word says, "Fear not, I am with you."

God says He is with me, "for I am your God." He Who created this world and me, must have the answers to my quandaries. On this widow journey I know there are shadows, steep climbs, tripping hazards, and dark valleys. Fear raises shadows of doubt: Can I do this? Who will be my sounding board, helping me process life? Will others take advantage and complicate my way as I struggle with this new path? Will I be ignored and alone? Where should I live? What's next? What challenges await me? Psalm 27:14

says, "Wait on the Lord; be strong and take heart and wait on the Lord." So, I will wait on His answers, His directions.

So, while I am waiting on His answers, I see that He will continue to strengthen me, help me, and grasping me with His righteous right hand. I'm so thankful for the Lord's presence, supporting, helping, steadying me as He leads me forward on this unknown terrain. Knowing this that He is Almighty, Omnipotent, Omniscient, Always-Present, Compassionate, Faithful, Loving, Sovereign, and Holy, as He is God. Who else could I believe to do this? Do not fear, for I am with you. Do not be afraid, for I am God. No one, really, only God. He Who fills all these attributes can replace the fear with His unfathomable peace.

He promises faithful strength and His assistance is holding me with His righteous right hand. Like crossing the highway of life, He is holding My hand. The path winds along a cliff, and He is holding My hand. The climb is steep and wearying, I know He is holding My hand. The night is long, the valley is dark, yes, He is right there holding My hand. And He is always present, calming my heart "Do not fear——do not be afraid, for I am your God."

Lord, My steps become less certain when I take my eyes off of Who You are. When I read Your promises to strengthen me, help me, hold onto me, I remember that You know what lies ahead of me. You've been there. You've already seen the terrain my widow path cuts through, so I can step with confidence where You lead. Steep ways, stormy days, dark valleys, Thank You for Your help. You've promised to never leave me nor forsake me. And because of Who You are, I can rest with assurance in You. In Jesus' Name, Amen.

> **Grief notes: It's advice often given to the newly bereaved to wait a year before making any big decisions. And that is likely true in most cases. With a new loss is a lot of grief fog and some paralyzed thinking. Take care of yourself, make order of what you can, but big purchases or selling your home require some major thinking. When you do, get trusted folks to walk through it with you.**

Journal 31

"I declare the end from the beginning and
from long ago what is not yet done, saying:
my plan will take place, and I will do all My
will." Isaiah 46:10

God's ways are so far above what I could ever attempt
to know or figure out. This tapestry of His will is so intri-
cate and detailed, yet I am in awe of the small part I see
being woven.

I know many Godly people prayed for Dan to recover,
for his healing, his survival. Yet he passed into Heaven. My
first reaction was "Why?" But I came to see that answer
was tucked into the great tapestry of God's design, a single
tinted thread tied off. God knows our last day before we've
lived one of them (Psalm 139:16). He knows the end from
the very beginning. His sovereign plan, the very DNA of
the universe, will happen. His will is on course, and nothing
can stop it. Deep and wide, the colors of His weaving, the
threads that bring shadow, depth, and detail, the woof and

the warp that run through many lives. Yet in His sovereign way, He will never waste a stitch. Where the needle passes over and under, lives are touched. Where the last of the thread is tied off, we don't know, and the impact we may never know until we see from Heaven's vantage point the completed fabric.

I still am in awe at the details He had worked out in what came to be the final years of Dan's life. Details so amazingly tied off and completed that there was no doubt that God had been working. It's now clear that God's will was playing out. Prayers were being answered, and we'd been so thankfully amazed! Properties sold and opportunities opened like never before! In looking back now, it seems obvious. Though I view it now through the haze of grief, I still recognize the kindness of God, the completeness of His work, and the generosity of His faithfulness.

And yes, I still ask questions. Not so much "Why?", but "What now?" I'm learning. He's known the end since the beginning, from long ago, what is not yet done, so I know His plan will take place and His will is certain to be done. I'm still here on earth, so He still has a plan for me, and He will lead me to accomplish that purpose for this widow path.

Lord, What You have ordained long ago is still taking place. I'm thankful for Your love, mercy, and faithfulness that is leading me. Your infinite wisdom has designed every step. As you continue working the threads of this life tapestry, I trust Your hands to guide the threads of colors of praise, worship, and joy that mingle with the shades of grief, heartache, and sadness. But in every detail of this journey, I lift them all to You. In Jesus' Name, Amen

> **Grief notes: For some, going back to church is difficult. It may stir up memories, or just seeing others sitting as couples or families will remind you of your loss. Finding another friend to sit with or sitting in a new area could help. Sometimes sitting near the back offers the possibility if it gets too difficult, you can slip out and try again next week.**

Journal 32

"I cry aloud to the Lord; I plead aloud to the Lord for mercy. I pour out my complaint before Him; I reveal my trouble to Him. Although my spirit is weak within me, You know my way." Psalm 42:1-3

I am remembering again today that grief is like an onion, tightly closed at first, then as reality sets in, the layers of the onion open up, unfolding to reveal new losses we begin to recognize. In losing Dan, what all have I lost? I've lost my best friend, father of my children, co-holder of 43 years' worth of memories, my co-adventurer, co-planner of house remodeling, my sweetheart, my source of "earthly comfort", my driver, my sounding board, my warmth on a cold night, prayer partner, the one I dressed for, my locus of wisdom for all things handyman and DIY, my Mr. Fix-it who could MacGyver any situation, my trip planner and so much more is identified as the "onion" opens.

Realizing the multiple losses, I also realize the new weakness that envelopes me. It sends me to my knees like the wind being knocked out of me. "I cry aloud to the Lord" pleading, pouring out my complaint, revealing my troubled heart. These new realities are too much. How can I ever replace what's gone? I open my Bible to the Psalms and I pray those Psalms that speak my pain and my heartache. Then, I read "My grace is sufficient for you" the Lord said, "for My strength is made perfect in weakness." Perfect strength for my sabotaging weakness when I need it most. I thought I had moved on, further away from the pain, but I bump into grief again.

Yes, time and again I've taken this weakness, these losses to the Lord and He's provided strength, comfort, and peace. The overwhelming "Yes, he's gone" mornings, the "firsts" all take their toll. Revisiting the account of Gideon's army brings encouraging words. The Lord kept paring down the soldiers until it would become evident to everyone that the victory would be the Lord's! I see what He's doing there; this is His own perfect strength and there is no doubt about it.

Yes, He knows what I need in my weakness, in my losses, in this expanding grief "onion". Yet He provides sufficient grace and perfect strength for my weakness. His grace gives me the victory that can only come through His provision. So as long as it takes to heal, I will continue to "pour out my complaints before Him." This new life He has called me to is one He has already charted. He knew the very day this season would begin. I didn't, but He knows my way.

Lord, I cry aloud to You for my every loss, my every need, my every weakness, for You know my sorrow as well as my needs. On my own, I get focused on me and lose sight of Victory in You. You know my past, my present, as well as my future. I trust You with what is to come along this widow path, for You know and You guide my way. In Jesus' Name, Amen

> **Grief notes: Children sometimes grieve with us. They see how we weep and should see that it's okay to shed tears. Talking about our beloved is ok. Look at pictures of them and our lost loved one. Recount the memories with them. Some create memory boxes with his items and photos of the child with their late father or grandpa. There are many resources available to help kids with grief, but I'd just caution that we look for ones that are spiritually safe.**

Journal 33

"You will keep the mind that is dependent
on You in perfect peace, for it is trusting in
You." Isaiah 26:3

Where I'm from in Oregon, there stood an old, dilap-
idated house in the country that I would pass on my way
to work. In fact, it was well-known, not so much for who'd
lived there, but the mere fact that it was still standing. It was
a two-story vacant farmhouse leaning on trees. Windstorms,
snowstorms, earthquakes all came and did not dislodge that
leaning house. It was tilting, dependent on those big old
trees that still surrounded it.

So much newness brings a heavy weight. In the closing
and opening of accounts, only my name is now on the
new checking account. Jumping through the hoops of regis-
tering the car in a new state, again all now in my name only.
Then some warning lights appear on my dashboard and a
wiper blade needed replacing. So many details that Dan
always handled, but it's my responsibility now. My mind

reels at times with so many changes like a wheel of misfortune. "You will keep in perfect peace those whose minds are steadfast because they trust (are confident and sure) in You."

Like a magnet, this verse keeps pulling me in. In fact, I've never felt so dependent on the Lord than in these months after Dan's passing. Many times, each day, and in the night, I come back to this promise: You will keep guarding the mind that is dependent on You, the one needing Your presence, requiring Your peace, desperate for Your strength. Keep it in some peace? A modicum of peace? No! In perfect peace! Why? Because that mind that tends to slide off the rails into the dark of lonely, into the ditch of Enemy lies "this is how awful it will be forever!" or "I can't do this!" This mind needs peace. Calm. Safety. The waves of grief hit, and the swells knock me down and threaten to carry me away.

But I am kept. He will keep the mind, the steadfast mind, the one that is leaned upon the Lord, trusting, fixed on and wholly dependent. This steadfast mind will be kept in perfect peace for it is trusting on and confident in the Sovereign One, the all-knowing, all-seeing, faithful, compassionate, Almighty Lord of Angel Armies. He's got me. He's got this. I may be clotheslined by grief, but in the strength of His promises, I can stand, and I can stand steadfastly, with a mind at peace and rest, leaning on Him. I'm like that old farmhouse, withstanding what comes, because I am braced in trust on the only One who can keep me.

Lord, Your promises keep me standing. I know You can calm the raging storms of grief and keep me at peace, because when I fix my mind on who You are, I know I am in eternally capable hands. I can trust all things to You. I am thankful Your promises never fail. And I commit to You the times that would undo me, were it not for Your perfect peace and strength I am leaning on. In Jesus' Name, Amen

Grief notes: Loneliness is part of grief because we have lost a life-partner. As you move forward, you might want to find a grief class at a local church, or you may want to get involved with some volunteer work in your community. These are small but mighty steps to find connection to others.

Journal 34

"Don't neglect to do what is good and to share, for God is pleased with such sacrifices." Hebrews13:16

Some days it seems I'm so self-focused on how I'm feeling. The hurt is chest-crushing at times, as the waves hit. I think: will this end? However, my dry mouth is getting better, I've discovered. My hair is still shedding, way too much to be in the normal range, whatever normal now is. I'm trying to improve on a bedtime that is before midnight and making sure I eat something at regular times. In this widow's "brain fog", what am I forgetting to do?

"Don't neglect to do what is good…" Dan loved to be generous. He said it was a testimony to others of Who God is, our lavish gift-giving Heavenly Father. Doing good for those around us and sharing wherever possible, these are sacrifices that please God. Dan loved using his building skills to help others, or even helping someone who ran into difficulties. He knew whatever we had, came from God, and that He would faithfully supply our needs. And even now, as Dan is with the Lord, I want to honor his memory, his life, and what brought him joy: I need to remember to find ways to be generous, and not forget the importance of doing what the Lord has put on my heart.

Well, of course I'm not a do-it-yourselfer, not a carpenter; I can boast no skills like Dan had, but there are some things I can do. So, I can brainstorm a list of ways to contribute at church, in the community, those in our families who need some help. Praying over the possibilities, I ask the Lord to lead in this way to show me opportunities to "do what is good and to share."

Yes, on this widow's journey, so much of life is new and different, yet I don't want to forget the foundational features that speak to who our family was in Christ. Grief can distract me, but life priorities that bring glory to the Lord are anchor points that draw me back to Him, who I am in Christ, and how to live in a way that moves me on toward a purpose of serving Him. Being generous with time, talents, and treasures can help me reach out of my own fog, to bring comfort and help to another person. And that is what would please the God of all comfort.

Lord, I pray You will lead me to the open doors and hearts that need You. Show me where I can be of service to You and guide me to honor my beloved's memory. Thank you for the opportunities You will lay on my heart for Your purpose for me going forward and may I be obedient in trusting Your leading to where there is need. In Jesus' Name, Amen.

> **Grief notes: It might seem easier to say, "I'm moving forward" than to say, "I'm moving on." Moving on may sound like moving on and away from the memory of our beloved. Moving forward sounds like progress. In moving forward, we can find ways to honor the memory of our beloved in a manner that shows some of their interests, talents, or personal service.**

Journal 35

"Those who sow in tears will reap with shouts
of joy. Though one goes along weeping, carrying the bag of seed, he will surely come
back with shouts of joy, carrying his sheaves."
Psalm 126:5-6

As I move along this widow's path, there comes a time
when I must step out of my safety "cave" and into the
commerce of the day. As a retired widow, I have not gone
back into any workplace, but there were some uncomfort-
able "firsts" this week. I went solo to Home Depot and to
Lowes. I knew there would be triggers, and I braced myself.
Remodeling and woodworking were in Dan's veins, so we
were in these home improvements stores a lot. And I do
mean a lot. I knew this trip was going to be challenging.
The aisles of tools, the smell of plywood, the sounds, it was
a memory mélange. Breathe. Focus on one thing. What am
I looking for? Walk to the check out.

Keeping my wandering mind in check, I will take the "poor me" thoughts captive. Tears can wait. I'll cry later. He's in Heaven, not needing 2x4's and drill bits. Then, there's a new focus: how many folks in the self-checkout line know Jesus? How could a person share Jesus here? What about the mama with the toddler and an infant in a carrier? My thoughts shift, and I know it's God refocusing me away from myself, away from the pain I could be drowning in. There are people, wherever I go, who do not know Jesus and if they'd been in Dan's situation, where would they be now? The thought crystallizes on my heart. There's work to be done. A lot of work. Time and opportunity and we are given one, we seize the other.

So, I go along and take opportunities to share Jesus. The homeless girl in the parking lot asks for some change. I had a few quarters and a tract about Heaven I shared with her and told her my husband had recently gone to heaven. She looked surprised I'd share that and told me her daddy was in heaven. I prayed with her right there at my car door. I shared John 3:16 with her and she quoted nearly the whole verse with me! Now it was my turn to be surprised! I see that God did there.

Sharing my bag of seed, we can find small ways to sow the Word into hearts here and there on our path. I look forward to the "sheaves", gathered one day to the

Lord Himself. And it might be, just maybe, that they had encountered someone in line at Home Depot or ordering lunch at Raising Canes who shared the Love Story of Jesus with them.

Lord, What a joy it is to share Jesus with others who need You more than they know. May I focus on sowing the seeds of the Gospel, even through my tears of loss, knowing You will guide my steps, my words, and give me wisdom. Direct me, Lord, to find the plan and purpose You have still for me, and where and how to serve You. In Jesus' Name, Amen

> **Grief notes: Heading to a place that is sure to be a trigger means we need to pre-plan our thinking. Find a focus that is part of the new you, your new way of thinking. If you fear tears, tell yourself your will find time later to weep over this place that holds trip-hazards of grief. And do it. In your place of solitude, let the tears fall.**

Journal 36

"So then, let those who suffer according to God's will entrust themselves to a faithful Creator while doing what is good." 1 Peter 4:19

Entrust. I entrust money to the bank. I entrust my trip to my car to get me safely there and back. I entrust flat rate boxes to the US Mail to wing their way from Texas to Alaska! Can I entrust myself to my faithful Creator? Immediately I say, "I must!" and then I look down at the path my feet are on. Not a path I chose, but the one God chose for me.

I'm realizing that this path is what God had planned for me, suffering the untimely, at least unexpected, loss of Dan being part of His holy plan for my life. Ouch. I understand this, that's not an easy first response. Even though this grief is hard, I am realizing that it's God at work here, so it brings some comfort. Because of who He is, I tell myself, I can trust Him. I can entrust my life and this new way to His keeping and direction.

Indeed, He's been with me from moment one. His Word, and His presence, have been a steady anchor in this storm. The apostle Paul urges those who suffer according to God's will to entrust themselves to a faithful Creator, relying on His immeasurable riches of grace, His constant kindness and love. Who else could I rely on? After all, He knows the dark suffering that took place at Calvary, the ultimate entrusting of the Son's life to the Father's wrath against sin, knowing this was the only way we could ever have salvation and eternal life in Heaven with Him.

Yes, if I believe this redirection to a widow's pathway has been God's will for my life, then my way forward is to entrust, commit, turn over and give custody of myself to Him, my faithful Savior. He's able to make a way when there seems to be no way. He is the Light that shines out of darkness, and the darkness could not overcome it. (John 1) He is the Way. In fact, He knows where He wants me to shine every day! As I entrust my days, I rely on the fact that He will show me the good that I should do.

Committing it all to Him, while doing the good He calls me to is a worthy goal. The fears creep in asking what should I do next? I will seek His direction daily and keep doing what He sends me to do and entrusting to Him my way forward.

Lord, I'm realizing this widow path is where You have placed me, so I entrust my way to You, the Way maker, the Way, Truth, and Life. I'm thankful for Your presence, Your peace, and the strength You provide daily. I ask for Your wisdom and grace to guide me to opportunities to do what is good in serving You, as I commit this path to You. In Jesus' Name, Amen

Grief notes: "I am mad at God" can be like the lament of "Why?" The Psalms are full of hard questions put to God. He is under no obligation to answer these, but as we look at His many names and characteristics, we begin to see Him in a new light. Mysteries are hidden with Him and only eternity will reveal our answers. For now, we can trust He is carrying out His divine plan. One stone in the water creates many ripples, so we don't know what impacts come from one loss and when He ordains it. We can only trust our sovereign God.

Journal 37

"I am the Lord's servant…May it be done
to me according to your word." Luke 1:38

I believe it was a holy, sovereign God who brought
Dan and I together 43 years ago, and this same omnipotent,
omniscient God answered our prayers, led, and guided us
over the span of our lives together. So, I must acknowledge
His sovereign hand in taking Dan home to Heaven at the
time He did, and the timing was His choice.

When the young virgin Mary replied to the angel, it
must have been on shaking legs of faith and obedience.
Nonetheless, she states, "I am the Lord's servant." Her service, to carry this special Messiah-child, was dedicated to
the Lord she knew was faithful. Nothing was or would ever
be impossible with the Lord. What the angel reported to her,
she agreed with it in implicit trust and obedience. Her road
ahead would be a challenge: a young Jewish girl, pregnant.
Her path ahead would not be without grief, prophesied by
Simeon at the temple, "A sword shall pierce your own soul."

(Luke 2:35) But step by step, she walked into that calling, trusting that God would remain faithful, true to His Holy Word delivered by the angel.

"May it be done according to your word." No angel appeared to me, but the wisdom of the scripture rang true in my heart. This path the Lord has set me on is His plan for me now. As I read the promises of God, that He was never leaving or forsaking me, that I can cast all my cares on Him, for He cares for me, and that He will keep me in perfect peace when I keep my mind steadfastly on Him, I must surrender to Him from here on, "May it be done according to Your word'. When I seek where to go, I hear Mary's response: May it be done according to Your Word. When I begin to wonder about what I should do, I will say, "May it be done according to Your Will."

Moving in faith when the way seems lined with sadness, reminders of loss, even in new storms of grief that surge unexpectedly, "I am the Lord's servant." I must remind myself: He is working. Even when I can't see it or feel it—-He is working. He always has, He always will. And may it so be done.

Lord, Your Way is Holy and known only to You. From the unprecedented to the unlikely, You are using instruments of change to bring about Your Will. Your grace, compassion, and kindness follow, and You still tell me to Trust even in this transition. As I try not to lean on my own understanding, I will acknowledge all You have done for us, for me. And I know You alone will direct my path. In Jesus' Name, Amen

> **Grief notes: Sometimes the woulda-shoulda thoughts get ahold of us and we experience guilt. Things we begin to think we should have done, things we wish we would have acted on, but we didn't, so now they are a source of guilt. I realized mine were baseless. They were more a product of faulty thinking than any effect my actions could have made better or changed the outcome. I had to confess and entrust them to God and let His grace be sufficient.**

Journal 38

"The Lord will send His faithful love by day;
His song will be with me in the night—a
prayer to the God of my life." Psalm 42:8

Life milestones always pose a challenge: those feared "firsts" after a loved one has been called home to Heaven. Birthdays, special days. Just the anticipation is hard enough, seeing that anniversary date approach on the calendar. I've dreaded it, as I see it inch closer. But time does not stop, and the day will arrive.

"The Lord will send His faithful love by day." Yes, even those days that feel like I'm facing an ice-breaker ship plowing my way, where I dread the memories that will descend upon me. Will I be hit mercilessly by a powerful grief surge? The anticipation, I'm finding, is often worse than the day's arrival, but I have this promise that He will send His faithful, constant, unswerving, and loyal love. And not only His faithful love by day, but His song by night, bringing peace to the storm, calm to the waters, and a hush to the fierce wind.

Yes, even in 2 a.m. moments I have His song with me in the night, in the dark of my soul, when I am most prone to wonder and my mind also goes wandering through the emptiness, the loneliness, the future, the why's, the what-may-come. His presence is a song that calms my ragged thoughts, and ushers in His deep abiding peace that reminds me He is here, He won't abandon me, He is faithful, and He cares. And He knows, like no one else because He has always been here.

His life-plan for me included this season of widowhood since He is the God of and designer of my life. So, this is how I can begin to see light on a path forward: A prayer to the strong God of my life, my support, my strength. I pray for His grace for the days to come, for who else could do what He alone can do? I choose to abide, remain in Him, for that is where life is, and this life is in His hands.

Good days and hard days, He sees them all. He also notices the anticipation that ties me in knots, so I offer that to Him as well. In committing these days to Him, I trust Him to make that way where I cannot see how to survive those life markers. He knows how the milestones, those seemingly never-ending "firsts" that will affect me. And He is there ahead of me, meeting me again in the hurt and disappointment, with His grace, sustaining all-sufficient grace, with faithful love and a song.

Lord, You know these days that would break me, but I also know You are there already, ready to meet me in my need. Your strength and grace will provide what my soul requires. God of all comfort, You are my relief. So, I again surrender these times to you, for they are already in Your hand. In Jesus' Name, Amen

> **Grief notes: Holidays can be tough days to get through, especially the first ones. Be kind to yourself. Plan ahead, if you can, to decide how you want to decorate that tree (or not), to attend a large family gathering (or not), or even how you intend to celebrate (or not).**

Journal 39

"Be satisfied with what you have, for He Himself has said 'I will never leave you or abandon you.' Therefore, we may boldly say the Lord is my helper, I will not be afraid."
Hebrews 13: 5-6

It's become so clear that the Enemy stalks us even in grief. He is indeed shameless and cruel. It really makes me examine where some of these waves of grief originate! Is this self-pity? Am I sad because poor me must take on a task I'd rather not and would've relegated to Dan were he still here? Does this wave of darkness reek of fear? Misgivings about the future? The "what-ifs"?

Yes, I can see where the Enemy sure seems to bring on the discouragement, the distraction, and the despair. I monitor my self-talk when I need a pep-talk! And where does the pep-talk come from? The Word of God! Starting with Hebrews 13:5-6, "Be satisfied with what you have." That's pretty straight forward! Stop pining for what is not, what will not be. You have a lot of blessings, so start counting them! You have a lot of promises from God, so read and memorize them! This is followed up with: "He Himself had said "I will never leave you or abandon you." God promised His constant faithful presence! "Therefore (that's why!) we may boldly say (even when I don't feel so bold) the Lord is my helper, I will not be afraid." Not afraid of the hoops necessary to jump through to start this new life in Texas. Not terrified of the gazillion steps to get my new Texas driver's license. Not fearful of wading into gathering a mountain of paperwork for doing Oregon and Texas taxes!

When the Enemy rolls the stone of discouragement into my widow's path, I recall this verse: 2 Peter 1:3,4: "His divine power has given us everything we need for a godly life through our knowledge of Him who called us by His own glory and goodness. Through these He has given us His great and precious promises, so that you can participate in the divine nature, having escaped the corruption in the world caused by evil desires." And that's good news to my heart. His divine power! Great and precious promises! That's a great match for the cruel and shameless one looking to throw me off balance with fear and discouragement.

In the Enemy's attempts to waylay my grieving process, I call to mind the ways God blessed us as a couple time and again. And I know He will be just as faithful to those promises when it's just me needing His strength, wisdom, and grace on this journey He's called me to step into. And yes, I can be satisfied with what I have, for I have Him, and His divine power through the Holy Spirit Who is reminding me of all the great and precious promises in His Word.

Lord, I know the enemy tries to draw me off course on this journey, but I also know You are the One in control. As I recall Your promise to be with me, and all the other many great and precious promises, I know Your divine power is giving me all I need to live a godly life. I have confidence in You and am thankful that the journey ahead of me is in Your hands. In Jesus' Name, Amen

> **Grief notes: Grief can sometimes bring on nightmares that re-experience the time before or immediately after our beloved's passing. Sometimes we even try to avoid sleep, so we don't dream. Praying and reading comforting Psalms at bedtime helps, and so does praying specifically for peaceful rest. Rest is important, so if that doesn't help, be sure to ask your doctor for advice.**

Journal 40

"I am deeply grieved to the point of death. Remain here and stay awake…Abba, Father! All things are possible for You. Take this cup away from me. Nevertheless, not what I will, but what You will." Mark 14: 34-36

Jesus knew deep to-the-point-of-sweat-like-blood grief. He asked His disciples to sit there while He prayed, to stay and remain awake. But the grief was not theirs. Jesus knew what lay ahead of Him: agony, separation from the Father, pain, death, and immense suffering. He also understood what lay ahead for these disciples, but they fell asleep anyway. They could not relate to His grief at that point. One day they would, but by then they'd be empowered by the Holy Spirit and their understanding of resurrection.

It's hard, if not impossible, for those around me to understand my grief. The loss of a spouse is so different from the loss of a parent, sibling, relative or friend. Only someone who has lost their spouse can relate to the feeling of amputation, to suddenly lose a lifelong relationship of two-becoming-one, then only one remains of the two. The depth of heartache seemed to lodge in my chest, making every breath heavy. Separated by the permanence of death, aloneness would steal over me as the reality began to dawn that this is all there is now.

And not for the last time, I'd remember Jesus' suffering which was unlike any other's pain, and the separation He experienced when God the Father turned His back on Him as He bore the punishment for sin, my sin. He felt separation. He felt alone. The heart's breaking as the plan of salvation played out there on the cross during those dark hours. The torture Jesus experienced at the hands of His crucifiers, the pain He endured as He, the spotless, sinless Lamb of God, took sin's punishment from His Father, the wages due to me, and the world.

But Sunday was coming. Three days later, Jesus arose from the dead and met with His disciples again. Over the course of 40 days, He was seen by over 500 folks, verifying He was alive. He'd conquered death by rising from the dead. And then, He went back to Heaven. He rose from the earth up to Heaven, with angels standing by. Suddenly the disciples were on their own. They weren't sleeping now. The Holy Spirit was about to make a powerful earthly entry into the hearts of those who believed this saving Good News.

Yes, realizing how God understands these new widow needs, can comfort me, and His peace and strength has become so real through His Word. Yet knowing all He went through to provide for my forgiveness and eternal welfare reminds me: He knows. My path ahead is set firm in Him because He understands where I've been, and where I'm going. I can rest in that. Forever.

Lord, Thank You for all of Salvation's plan and the hope You secured for every believer. You understand my hurting more than anyone. I know my steps forward in healing are all in You. In Jesus' Name, Amen

> **Grief notes: Some folks will say that grief will just take time to get over. I don't think that's accurate. Some folks who don't work on their grief are still suffering years later. It's best to talk it out, pursue a grief group, and learn how to turn your suffering over to the Lord each day, and let Him restore your soul.**

Journal 41

"Though I am surrounded by troubles, You preserve my life…The Lord will fulfill His purpose for me. The Lord will work out His plans for my life, for Your faithful love endures forever." Psalm 138:8 (NLT)

At least it seems like troubles when the low tire warning light keeps coming on and the Maintenance Required icon keeps reminding me it's time for an oil change. Sometimes those dashboard lights of life light up, too! You didn't get enough sleep! You didn't eat enough! It seems like the perfect time to open my Bible and read a Psalm. Now more than ever, I need to pay attention to those warning lights, otherwise I find it harder and harder to cope. My strength retreats and the weight of the past months comes rushing in, and every time my faith takes a hit.

Now is when I need to make sure I've eaten right, rested adequately, and have fed my soul on the hope-filled Word of God. Now is when I need to dial up the praise music and worship His Holy name. He preserves my life and promises

His constant faithful presence and His compassion that restores my soul. Reading again of who He is reinforces my faith and reminds me that I know He has a sovereign plan and purpose for my life. It prompts me to realize anew that He is righteous and kind (Psalm 145:17). That He alone is unchanging (Malachi 3:6). That He is able to do all things and no purpose of His can be thwarted (Job 42:2). There is nothing that is too hard for Him (Jeremiah 32: 17). He is our eternal refuge, and His everlasting arms are underneath me. (Deuteronomy 33:27). And although I may not know what His purpose is for me at this moment, I trust Him to lead me to serve in ways He's preparing me for. Just realizing who God is reinforces my faith and restores my hope. I know He can handle my needs. He is worthy of all trust, so I make that choice. Trust Him.

In addition to reading the Word of God, I need to be in His presence in prayer, so I can use the PRAY acronym: Praising Him for all He had done to provide for me: salvation, daily needs, rest, the love of family and friends. I need to Repent for ways I failed Him, going my own way, relying on my own thinking, pushing on in my own strength. I must Ask for needs for family, loved ones, and my requests going forward. Then, I need to Yield to His Sovereign will for my life, and for the future. P-R-A-Y is a nice acronym to help guide and strengthen my time in prayer.

The Lord will work out His plans for this widow journey. As I ask for His wisdom along this pathway, I am sure. I'm James 1:5-sure! If I lack wisdom, He will provide when I ask, and it will be given. Because His faithful love is enduring forever, I am convinced His work for me will last until my path is complete.

Lord, I know I need to keep an eye on my "dashboard." Sometimes I lose track of my rest, my eating, my anxious thoughts and my spiritual food, as well. Lord, You are faithful and loving and I trust and thank You that You will fulfill Your purpose for me and work out the plans for my life in ways to serve You. In Jesus' Name, Amen

> **Grief Notes: Keep an eye on your dashboard! Getting overtired is not healthy and you will be more apt to cave in emotionally. Pace yourself, keep a check on how much you take on and how many activities you have going on. Declining an invite for some needed rest might be a better choice.**

Journal 42

"But the one who boasts should boast in this:
that he understands and knows me—-that I
am the Lord, showing faithful love, justice,
and righteousness on the earth for I delight
in these things." Jeremiah 9:24

As I walk this new journey of widowhood, I want others
to know how I can deal with life now: it's all because of the
Lord. There would not be light on this pathway without
His presence! His promises, His presence, His comfort, and
peace, those have all been provided by my Lord. From my
first waking moments to my turning to Him in prayer when
I click off my bedside light, it's Jesus. The words that inspire
me: His. The music I choose to listen to (yes, Choose!):
His praise. The books I read: inspiration from Him. Am I
boasting? It's interesting that that word boast means "shine".
If I am "shining" something in my life, reflecting the One
who is my Light in the darkness, I want it to be Jesus.

"That he understands (has intellect, wisdom) and knows me…" The more I rely on God's wisdom and direction for this new path, and the more I learn and know Who He Is, it builds my faith and trust in Him. I understand more of His Character, His all-powerfulness, all-knowing, unchanging nature and I am assured that He is the same yesterday, today, forever.

"That I am the Lord, showing faithful love, justice, and righteousness on the earth…" These are reliable character traits for a God I'm asking questions of and depending on. Daily. Hour by hour. I can't find that faithful love-justice-righteousness anywhere here on earth, but God reveals His sacred why He shows these to us: "for I delight in these things."

Yes, God delights in showing us faithful love. That's often hard to find among the best of friends. He loves us eternally, from eternity past to eternity future. He delights in Justice, that divine perspective of what is lawful, and that is not the definition the media or the world would distract us with. He delights in Righteousness, which is rightness, according to His divine standards, not the changing whims of mankind tainting divine authority regarding what is currently perceived as right or wrong.

So, if I'm to shine on this path, it will be because Jesus is providing the light. I want to understand and know the

Lord's purpose for me, and to walk in the ways in which He delights. One step at a time. One valley at a time. One mountain at a time.

Lord, I submit this path to You. Nothing that's brought me this far is anything I can boast about—only Your faithful love. May I continue to seek where You lead, to know You more, and be led by what brings You delight. In Jesus' Name, Amen

> **Grief notes: Be sure you are the one sharing your story, not others telling it for you through their filter. This is the story you know and that you've experienced, so make sure you are the one telling your story.**

Journal 43

"The Lord is compassionate and gracious, slow to anger and abounding in faithful love. But from eternity to eternity the Lord's faithful love is toward those who fear Him and His righteousness toward the grandchildren of those who keep His covenant, who remember to observe His precepts." Psalm 103:8; 17-18a

There is a real legacy in the Lord that parents and grandparents can leave to their children and grandchildren. Dan was an incredible dad and grandpa, an honest, loving, hardworking guy who loved the Lord. His grands miss him and how he loved spending time with them, but they know that he is in Heaven. Every day we spent time covering our children and our grandchildren together in prayer and it's a habit I am committed to continue. So, I'm encouraged when I read this promise that He is faithful to our future generations.

What an amazing list of God's attributes whom we love and serve. This incredible faithful love is from eternity to eternity! Everlasting to everlasting! Always and Always! That's forever! This faithful love is forever toward those who have reverence toward Him. And His righteousness, His righteous acts, His justice, keeping His promises, all these extend to children's children. Our future generations will be prayed over and taught by those who keep obeying His precepts. These are the very principles to be imprinting on the hearts of future generations, that we serve a compassionate, gracious, faithful Lord.

What a calling a widow with children and grandchildren has upon her life! Sharing the hope that is within us with the next generation is not just a nice idea, it's necessary for the blessing of our families and honors the legacy of our believing husbands! Pointing our children and grands to Christ, His salvation, and living for Him can become our mission, our purpose. As I see it, there's no better example for children and grandchildren than to see and hear a mother or grandmother relate how the Lord is her strength and peace.

To observe a surviving parent's faith becomes stronger through the trial and transition of grief can be a powerful witness to the keeping, comforting, strengthening power of our Savior. This can be an indelible memory for the family that through it all, you found that the Lord was enough. May our faithful love reflect His eternally compassionate, faithful love.

Lord, I want my children and grandchildren to know that You are a God abounding in faithful love. I pray daily for their salvation and walk with You. May they see in my journey that I trust You, that Your Word can guide them through life regardless of what they may face. I commit each of them to You and Your eternal purposes for their lives. In Jesus' Name, Amen.

> **Grief notes: Little by little, I realize that since I no longer have a husband to depend on, I can depend on God even for the little things! I can even ask Him for help getting the stubborn lid off the salad dressing! He can answer with an idea that works!**

Journal 44

> "I pray that from His glorious, unlim-
> ited resources He will empower you
> with inner strength through His Spirit."
> Ephesians 3:16 NLT

I pray for strength often these days. I know when weakness hits, I need power, power to move forward, power to stand, and power to take on new tasks and responsibilities. This kind of strength only comes from the Lord. Whether it's the ambushes, the triggers, the milestones I dread, I'm so thankful that He can grant this essential strength from the deep pockets of His magnificent infinite resources, through His Holy Spirit.

Unlimited resources for inner strength are some of the ways He gives me help. How? Through His Spirit. The Comforter Who is now God abiding in us, reminds us deep within our own spirit that He is present. In our lack, He gives of Himself over and over: immeasurable peace beyond our understanding of how this even works or even the miracle that it continues to flow. He provides grace that is sufficient and sustaining. His words come alive, soothing, answering, yielding a harvest of wisdom, and light for the path forward. These are eternal resources, a bottomless well of provision from God's abundance.

Isaiah 40:31 says, "They who hope in the Lord will renew their strength. They will soar on wings like eagles; they will run and not grow weary; they will walk and not be faint." This promise of renewed strength, eagle strength, gives hope for my bone-weary days. He also gives gentle reminders when the day becomes too much. His Holy Spirit reminds me that I need to rest, stay hydrated, nourished, and turn to Him when I feel anxious and overwhelmed.

Yes, letting my eyes focus on the hazards of the path before me, I can lose sight of the treasures in God's storehouse. I can forget in the distraction of the day the availability of the Holy Spirit to strengthen my heart and my feet for the way ahead that He has called me to. May I never forget the power of God to act! Paul also prompted the Ephesians to recall (1:18-20) "I pray that your hearts will be flooded with light so you can understand the confident hope He has given those He called...that you will understand the incredible greatness of God's power…this is the same mighty power that raised Christ from the dead…" (NLT) So, as God has "called" me to this new journey of being a widow, He will empower me for all the "new" He calls me to.

Lord, I praise You for the strength You have made available to me when I stumble, when weariness and faintness cloud my view of what unlimited resources are available in You. When my spirit is weak, I know I can hope in You for eagle strength. Your Holy Spirit hears my spirit's needs when I cannot say the words, but You understand, and send strength that only You know about. I commit these thin days to You, days when my strength is small, and need is great. I am thankful that only my All-knowing, All-seeing Sovereign Creator understands. In Jesus' Name, Amen

Grief notes: Traveling alone after loss can be a challenge. If it's usually been both of you traveling, flying alone can be interesting. Going through security alone, take your time. Take some time beforehand to check the airport's website for any changes. Be prepared to see couples and families that may trigger memories and be ready to thank God for all the times you'd enjoyed traveling together.

Journal 45

"If the God we serve exists, then He can
rescue us from the furnace of blazing fire,
and He can rescue us from the power of you,
the king. But even if he does not rescue us…
we will not serve your gods." Daniel 3:17-18

Even if. These were high stakes for the three young
men from Judah. They wouldn't bow to the statue of the
king of Babylon. They would only bow in worship to the
One True God, so for that they were cast into the fiery furnace. "If the God we serve exists, then He can rescue us…."
They had faith in the God they worshiped, even if those
around them did not. If He's real, He can rescue. They
didn't know if it would be God's will to act. "And He can
rescue us from the power of you, the king." They believed
God was able to deliver them from this fearful king "But
even if He does not rescue us…we will not serve your gods."
Whether or not, their conviction stood, and their obedience

remained firm. They would not worship anyone other than the Lord their God.

Even if. Those words are branded into my heart and soul. Even if I prayed that Dan would be healed, and even if the Lord chose to take him home to Heaven, even if it means I walk solo the rest of my days on earth with no other companionship than the Lord, I will continue to trust the Lord. Regardless of how God answered prayer for Dan's recovery, He has chosen this path for me. I know I will never be alone.

I know I won't be alone, like the story of Shadrach, Meshach and Abed-Nego, there was a fourth in the fiery furnace walking with them. It was One who appeared as the Son of God. Their bodies were not burned, their hair wasn't singed, their coats had not caught fire, and amazingly, there wasn't even the smell of smoke on them! Miraculous! Walking through life difficulties sometimes leaves elements of a "scent" of bitterness, disappointment, discouragement. However, as I begin this widow journey, I pray that I will not lose sight of all the Lord has called me to in His Holy Will, a Sovereign plan. His ways and thoughts are higher than mine, and I'm convinced of His promise to never leave nor abandon me. Perhaps most importantly, His grace is sufficient for me, for His strength is made perfect in my weakness.

Lord, Your plan is Holy and Sovereign, so as I again commit my way to You. I am thankful for Your constant presence. Sometimes this fiery furnace of grief seems unbearable, but I trust Your leading in this trial. Even if the burdens seem unbearably heavy at times, I know You can be trusted. You go before me, and all things come from Your righteous hand. Lead me and direct me as I submit this new path to You. In Jesus' Name, Amen.

> **Grief notes: Entering widowhood is a life transition. We plan for so many other transitions: college, marriage, parenthood, retirement, but becoming a widow is one we often pushed aside to "think about later".**

Journal 46

"For it is God who is working in you both
to will and to work according to His good
purpose." Philippians 2:13

God is working. He's always working. As the song says,
even when we don't see it, He's working. So, it appears He
is working in me both to design and to act according to
or on behalf of His good purpose. As the Amplified Bible
states: "For it is [not your strength, but it is] God who is
effectively at work in you, both to will and to work [that is,
strengthening, energizing, and creating in you the longing
and the ability to fulfill your purpose] for His good pleasure.
Amazing! He is at work in me to energize and make me want
to do this purpose He designed for me! He is even providing
the power and equipping me to do what He wants intends
for me to do.

When I reflect on the months before and after losing
Dan, I can see the Lord's hand at work, tracing the way He
was preparing me even before loss. His good purpose was

in motion, from property sales, to downsizing, and all our belongings already packed and in storage! Every bill and account at our previous residence, paid and closed. I mean, I could go down to the minutia of even an airline with a direct flight from Fairbanks, AK to Dallas, TX! No detail was spared. God was at work. The "new season" he and I were anticipating was not the one that was to be. God had other sovereign plans.

This new path has come with a new level of trust in God and realizing His way is best. I am choosing to trust, even when it's hard. I find I am leaning into His promises like never before. Philippians 4:13 has all new meaning: "For I can do everything through Christ, who gives me strength." I found strength with this scripture in just managing to fly from Fairbanks to Dallas a week after Dan's passing. Widow fog is real, but He led me and gave me the stamina I needed. Proverbs 3:5, 6 also took on fresh importance: "Trust in the Lord with all your heart and do not depend on your own understanding (Yes, that widow haze and fickle feelings can play tricks on your own understanding!) Seek His will in all you do, and He will show you which path to take." (NLT) What a promise! He will show me the path He has designed for me to take!

God is working in my life. In fact, He's been working on my life for many years. The same way He worked on both Dan and I, He is continuing His faithfulness on this path for me going forward. He will direct me, energize me, strengthen me, and prepare me for this journey that He is laying on my heart.

Lord, I surrender to You this path where You are directing me. This journey is the will and work You will guide me into and through to accomplish what is Your good purpose for me going forward. Thank You for all Your promises that light my way and provide strength for whatever comes next. In Jesus' Name, Amen

> **Grief notes: Friendships can be different after losing your husband. You are no longer part of a "couple", so couple friends may find it different to relate to you. It may be a reminder of what may come to them in time. Or it may simply be that you and the wife were friends, and the husbands had things in common, and now it's just you. Maybe consider adding new acquaintances with other single or widowed gals.**

Journal 47

"Do not fear, for I have redeemed you. I have
called you by your name, you are Mine. I
will be with you when you pass through the
waters and when you pass through the rivers,
they will not overwhelm you." Psalm 43:1-2

I am overwhelmed by God's amazing provision for
comfort and strength. He is truly the champion of widows!
In these past months, I've called on Him so many times. I've
reached for His Word countless times. Words that remind
me of His Sovereignty over life and His Presence with me.
Those words remind me again of His love, His purpose for
me going forward, and His precious promises that mean life
and peace at my worst moments.

Like today, when I realize it's one of the "lunaversaries"
which is one of the months' date marking the anniversary
of a special event, in this case of Dan's passing. It brings
vivid memories to the forefront that still sting. I even note
the time on the clock, digital images emblazoned my mind.
Images, words, feelings rush in like a sneaker wave. And

yes, the Enemy tries to wriggle in with guilt, doubt, and feelings of failure.

So, I meet those incursions of the Enemy with recalling that I am so blessed because the Lord has called me by my name. He says I am His. It's my identity. Even when passing through the trials of waters that would flood my heart and soul and through the raging rivers. Even where the currents of grief, fear, sadness, and the aches of longing might crush me, I know He is with me, giving peace. He administers comfort. Providing strength. He is truly a life preserver of hope, and He's kept His eye on me.

God's promise? These crushing waves won't overwhelm me. These deep waters won't devastate me. This loss was okayed by Him. He knew it was coming. Not only did He see it coming, but He also knows what's ahead of me yet. And He tells me not to fear. He's redeemed me. Purchased me. So, He owns me, right here where I am, journeying this path He's put me on.

It's not "if I pass through the waters" or "in case you pass through the rivers," it's when. There will be high-water times. He's building strength in me as I tread these rivers. It's the strength that comes when I realize that it originates in my time with Him in His Word, and in prayer. This is when the promises take root, His words of encouragement, and reminders to trust every care, thought, and situation to Him. Don't fear.

Months come and go. The wince of pain and loss reminds me that in many ways, I will always need Him. I don't need to fear these anniversaries because He will be with me. Always. And if He brings me to the waters, He will provide the lifeboat or the path through the stormy sea.

Lord, I praise You for the promises of Your presence, to be with me in the struggles, when the storms and currents of life threaten to overwhelm me. Thank You for redeeming me through Your Son, my Savior. May I share this hope and comfort daily with others who need Your peace. In Jesus' Name, Amen

> **Grief notes: There are anchors for us in grief and they are found in God's Word. We have taken a direct hit to our peace, hope, strength, and help. Storms of grief threaten us, but the sooner we find those anchors in His Word that remind of us how He keeps us, the better we can face the tempest.**

Journal 48

"I will bless the Lord who counsels me—
even at night when my thoughts trouble
me." Psalm 16:7

Nights are still tough. I want to rest, but I don't want
to dream. Dreams involving Dan leave me wrecked for
hours. I tend to stay up late, reading, watching faith videos
until I can barely keep my eyes open, then I drift off to
overdue sleep. Some nights I'm lying awake until the wee
hours, which is no way to calm an overactive, grieving mind!
Scenarios and what-ifs drift between memories and our final
moments, replaying in my head and twisting my heart.

I find I can turn to prayer when the clock keeps pro-
gressing and sleep has vanished. I know the Father is up all
night anyway, so I pray for peace for my rattled mind. I pray
for strength to move past this moment of swirling events
that I cannot change. Ever. I pray for grace—grace to accept
where God has placed me, what is undoubtedly His sovereign plan. His Word says His grace is sufficient for me, His

strength made perfect in my weakness. I feel weak in this wakeful hour, so I pray His strength will carry me toward the rest I know I need. Psalm 55:22 says to cast my burden on the Lord, and He will sustain me; He will never allow the righteous to be moved. Psalm 73: 26 (a favorite!) says my flesh and my heart may fail, but God is the strength of my heart and my portion forever! Jesus said, in John 14:27, "My peace I give to you, I don't give as the world gives. Do not let your hearts be troubled and do not be afraid." So, I pray the Word, the promises God has given to Champion my needs.

I continue praying. My thoughts turn toward others. I pray for those who also need the Lord's help like other members of my grief group. I pray for those who are battling illness, cancer, disease. I pray for family members and friends who do not yet know Christ as their Savior, as well as those who have walked away from faith, that they will be restored. I ask the Lord for guidance and wisdom how I can share Christ that day. Somewhere. Even a small deed that will point to the hope inside of me.

And by then, I'm usually ready to fall into sleep. With the wise counsel of His word, and the Counselor abiding within me, I can bless the Lord for He will keep me, my heart, my troubled thoughts and preserve the peace He's given for my rest.

Lord, When my mind is dealing with troubling thoughts and grief, You counsel me through Your word, helping me take captive those impressions that would rob me of rest. Thank You for the Counselor Who dwells within me and helps call to mind those precious promises of Your presence. In Jesus' Name, Amen

> **Grief notes: Sometimes anger erupts within us, at times aimed at our beloved. It might happen when we're faced with a new task we've never had to do. We are building skills our husbands would be proud of, but sometimes it is the last straw that prompts a meltdown. Be kind to yourself, realize God is your Champion now, and He is right there with you.**

Journal 49

"Cast your burden on the Lord, and He will sustain you; He will never allow the righteous to be shaken." Psalm 55:22

Every day, in fact, many times a day, I'm finding a new and different burden to cast on the Lord! When the memories get too heavy, when I start unpacking boxes from our move that sit in storage, reminders of what I thought would be our new season, I cast those burdens, cares, and soul-tears onto the Lord. His way of dealing with these simply reinforces what I've known for so long but only now am I truly realizing and appreciating His Almightiness!

Daily I'm amazed at His sustaining grace. His strength and support have kept and preserved me in countless ways. His Word is my strength, that reassurance of knowing He is in control, and I can submit each crisis to His knowing hand. I can rely on Him. Trusting Him is like breath. I rely on filling my spiritual lungs with the breath of who He is, the promises of His word, and His presence moment by moment. He quiets my restless heart, the aching doesn't just disappear, but He tenderly guides, shows me scripture that pours all new meaning over my soul to soothe and restore.

The enemy isn't like this. He sneaks around, bombarding me with condemnation and doubt. He plants thoughts of inadequacy and tries manipulating memories to cast dirt and despair on my peace of mind. He's a master at his stealth and knows his timing, dredging up old wounds, old scars. He knows ways to try and shake me, for a while.

But the Word says, "He will never allow the righteous to be shaken." Right there. For those of us looking to Him, insulating our hearts and minds with His promises, His character, His traits, He won't allow enemy shenanigans. I must let His word rule. His Word reminds me in 2 Corinthians 10:5 to take every thought captive to make it obedient to Christ. I remember Romans 8:1 says "No condemnation now exists for those in Christ Jesus." And then there's Philippians 4:8, "Whatever is true, whatever is honorable and worthy of respect, whatever is right and confirmed by God's word, whatever is pure and wholesome, whatever is lovely and brings peace, whatever is admirable and of good repute; if there is any excellence, if there's anything worthy of praise, think continually on these things [center your mind on them, and implant them in your heart]."

Yes, I may quake some days, there may be jolts that threaten me, but my future is steady in Christ. Life will be different, this is new territory, but I'm not alone. Others have passed on this path, and others are yet to come. But what a comfort it is to know I can cast these burdens on Him with the promise that He will sustain me.

Lord, Thank You that Your sustaining grace and mercies are new every day and they are mine. Direct my feet along this new pathway and help me to remember that Your Word is a lamp and a light for my journey. In Jesus' Name, Amen.

> **Grief notes: Complications can make grief harder to walk through. If you notice you are lingering for years in what feels like fresh, raw grief, consider seeking a Christian professional to help you sort out your feelings.**

Journal 50

"Who can separate us from the love of Christ? Can affliction or distress or persecution or famine or nakedness or danger or sword? …No, in all things we are more than conquerors through Him Who loved us." Romans 8:35-37

Everyone wants a sure thing such as a dependable car, a washing machine that lasts a decade, or a lawnmower that roars to life after a long winter. Guarantees, warranties, and purchase protection plans all try to reassure us that we bought a long-lasting product. But in the end, most things wear out and fail with time and use except for one thing. One eternal thing.

What is that one thing we can depend on for all time? The love of Christ. The unconditional, never failing, always present, protective, faithful, conquering love of Christ. And nothing, yes, nothing, can separate us from this love. Can losing your spouse make this love fail? No. In all the sorrow, loss, memories that make widows sad and long for happier days, and not even the mighty waves of grief can separate us from Him, because we are more than conquerors through Him who gave us this love in the first place!

In Jesus we have victory over these times when the enemy would like to bury us in pity for our dire situation. How could a loving God dare take our beloved husband, leaving me broken and alone, the enemy whispers to us. It's not fair, he continues, forget your faith! What good has it brought and now look where you are!

No, in all things, even vicious and cruel enemy attacks, we are more than winners through Christ. Through Christ, I know I have access to the Father, the comfort and help of the Holy Spirit, and the love of a Savior who willingly experienced the Cross to provide salvation because He loves me. Me! The new widow, still on shaky legs of this new walk God has called me to. The enemy may scheme to make me think my life is over, but he's wrong because he's been defeated through the One who conquered death.

Yes, we are more than conquerors. There is victory. In fact, Philippians 4:13 backs that up: "For I can do everything through Christ, who gives me strength." And then there's Isaiah 40:31 "But those who hope in the Lord will renew their strength. They will soar on wings like eagles; they will run and not grow weary; they will walk and not be faint." No one can separate us from the love Christ has for this new journey, for he provides the strength that nothing else can.

Lord, Thank You for the victory I have in You, for You alone provide conquering power, regardless of my circumstances. Thank You for the promises in Your word that strengthen me. I am not alone in this struggle and pain. I ask understanding and wisdom for the steps forward as I rely on Your faithful help and guidance I know I will need. In Jesus' Name, Amen.

> **Grief notes: Sometimes reaching out to comfort someone else who is grieving also helps our own healing process.**

"As for me, I vow that I will not sin against the Lord by ceasing to pray for you. I will teach you the good and right way. Above all, fear the Lord and worship Him faithfully with all your heart; consider the great things He has done for you." I Samuel 12:23-24

I am encouraged by the words of Samuel when he addresses the people of Israel after they asked for and received a king so they could be like other nations. He was disappointed, but his wisdom and kindness came through clearly: "Don't turn away from following the Lord. Instead, worship the Lord with all your heart. Don't turn to follow worthless things; they are worthless. The Lord will not abandon his people, because of His great name and because He has determined to make you His people." (1 Samuel 12:20-22)

Sometimes grief makes widows turn to look for what will help the hurt in any way possible. Some say they can't make it without a man in their life! This aloneness is killing them! They just want to be a couple again. They want that comfort; they need someone alongside them. Some want to numb the hurt, and so they turn to substances that do more harm than good. As Samuel wisely said, "Don't turn to follow worthless things—they are worthless."

So, where do I find what is worthy? "Above all, fear – with awe and profound reverence—and serve Him faithfully with all your heart, for consider what great things He has done for you." (Amp). When we take our eyes off of Him and all He has done for us, we soon start judging our life by the world's standard: "I want that (fill in the blank!) what "everyone" else has! I want to replace what He took away!

But Samuel says something interesting here: he makes a promise, a vow. "I vow that I will not sin against the Lord by ceasing to pray for you…" He knew where the longing to submit to God's plan would come from: a faithful heart, a heart that truly wants to honor the Lord. I love knowing that someone is praying for me!

And it's the same for widows. It's the faithful, trusting heart, seeking God in all the upheaval of grief that chooses to trust the Lord and realizes God won't abandon us! It's a promise! He knows my heart better than I do! I won't try to choose another "King" to follow! I must allow my heart to consider all the great things He's done for me! He has determined to be faithful to me! I pray for others' comfort and peace, too. I also pray I will find my value and purpose in our loving Savior. "But first and most importantly seek (aim at, strive after) His kingdom and His righteousness (His way of doing and being right—the attitude and character of God) and all these things will be given to you also." Matthew 6:33 (Amp) He knows me, and He certainly knows how I can serve Him. I can trust Him to fulfill the purpose to which He's leading me.

Lord, May I seek the right and the good way to bring honor to You. Thank You again for Your faithful promises and faithful leading. In Jesus' Name, Amen

> **Grief notes: Find ways to encourage others as you see the need. Looking outside our own pain, find a way to be a "boulevard of blessing, not a cul de sac of care". If you've been encouraged, pass on the blessing by sending a text or a note to someone who may need some sunshine today.**

Journal 52

"Thanks be unto God for His indescribable
gift." 2 Corinthians 9:15

Surviving the first Thanksgiving after Dan's passing
was interesting. It was the "first" holiday of the season that
starts all year-end, year-beginning holidays. The special days
where missing loved ones are really missed, and memories of
past holidays take up much more mental real estate than is
comfortable. With so much of social media consumed with
listing what we are grateful for, I happened upon this verse.

Simple, but in eight words, it reflects the boundless,
limitless mercies and grace that God has poured over me in
the last few months. (In reality, my whole life.) Thank God.
Thank God for His too-wonderful-for-words gift. Thank
God for responding to my tears and brokenness, dissolving
in the middle of the night, and yet pulling me back together
to make phone calls, do business that needed to be done,
and go places I needed to be.

Thank God. Thank God Dan was ready to meet Him on that night, hours after learning he wouldn't survive Covid pneumonia, and all had been done to help his virus-damaged lungs. Thank God that we had completed remodeling and sales of both our homes and properties. God knew the future, although we didn't. He'd seen to it that details were tied up and finished. Every. Single. One. Indescribable.

Thank God. Thank God that He sent His Son, Jesus, to be the sacrifice for sin, and victoriously conquered death, providing not only a home in Heaven, but the Holy Spirit of Truth to indwell every believer. Every. One. Of. Us. And He calls us His. His children. Indescribable.

Thank God. Thank God we have the promise of His presence, never leaving or abandoning us, as well as new mercies daily, peace with Him, and comfort, from the God of all comfort. We have hope, and a future. And then? Eternity in Heaven. Indescribable.

Yes, really: Thanks be to God for His indescribable Gift. Unutterable. Unspeakable. Inexpressible. Jesus Christ. He was the Gift and truly was and is the Way, the Truth, the Life.

Lord, I want to remember all the ways You are leading me through this transition . I am thankful for Your presence, Your hope, Your peace, and the relief You provide. You strengthen me in my weakness when I call to You and guide me along this new path. Lord, as I give the unknown twists and turns to You. I realize all my blessings are because of Jesus. May I continue to rely on You and see Your hand in all things. In Jesus' Name, Amen.

> **Grief notes: Spiritual warfare is real in grief. Be alert. The prowling Enemy wants to make you believe God cannot be trusted and will bring the worst deception at the worst time. Remember this: God has supplied the armor. He wants you to give all those struggles to Him.**

Journal 53

"I give thanks to Christ Jesus our Lord who
has strengthened me, because He considered me faithful…" I Timothy 1:12

Like everyone who encounters grief, there are often
unanswered "why" questions, followed by wondering "what
now?". Then I came upon this part of the verse: "because
He considered me faithful…"

There are questions I'll never know the answers to until
Heaven. I have known over the past months of grief and loss
that He has provided His strength in my times of weakness,
and He has given His wisdom in my wondering. God has
shown me His peace when misgivings gnawed at my rest.
I've also known the God of all comfort staying near this
broken heart, tenderly binding up my crushed spirit, and
providing hope where there seemed none. And I thank Him
for His faithful care, always championing, defending, and
protecting the widow (Psalm 68:5)

But then I read this: "He considered me faithful…" The
Lord okayed this event, Dan's passing, knowing the ordeal

ahead of me, His sovereign plan. Like Job, the enemy said Job would curse God, and God knew otherwise. Yet the suffering was real. Mr. and Mrs. Job experienced the loss of an entire family and all they owned. God knew Job's tensile strength would be stretched and tried. And He knew Job, maybe better than Job knew himself. God had considered Job's faithfulness, Job's stubborn refusal to turn against Him in his grief, affliction, and loss. Wiped out and hurting, surrounded by unhelpful advice, Job clings tenaciously to his faith in God. It was how God had known it would go. He had considered that Job, through it all, would be faithful to Him.

What an example to be drawn to. Did God look down through the ages and see that even if He took Dan to Heaven, I would find my strength in Him? Did He build into me over the years, the seeds of a faith that would turn to Him for my needs, my comfort, and my peace? He must've seen that I'd turn to Him for this journey on this widow's path. As Paul says to Timothy, the Amplified Bible says it well: "I thank Christ Jesus our Lord, who has granted me (the needed) strength and made me able for this, because He considered me faithful and trustworthy, putting me into service (for this ministry)."

Yes, God's granted me strength at times I knew I had none of my own, and made me able to go on, hour by hour, day by day, and week by week. He put me on this path, and where He guides, He provides the strength to keep going and sufficient grace for each situation. I've come to see how faithful He is, how close He is, and so I know I can keep relying on Him. I can keep trusting Him for everything because I want Him to continue to find me faithful to Him, to the purpose He's calling me to.

Lord, Thank You for Your faithfulness, Defender, Provider, Protector of the Widow. I know I am where You want me to be, in Your sovereign plan. As I continue to rely on You, may I be found faithful to this calling on my life. In Jesus' Name, Amen.

Grief notes: Grief is a place we are right now, but it doesn't have to be who we are. We grieve the loss and will always have a place of love in our hearts for our beloved, but as we move forward with God's healing and leading, we find ways to honor them and grow into this new transition to who He's calling us to be.

Journal 54

"Remember my affliction and my home-
lessness, the wormwood and the poison.
I continually remember them and have
become depressed. Yet I call this to mind,
and therefore I have hope: because of the
Lord's faithful love we do not perish, for His
mercies never end." Lamentations 3: 19-22

I remember. Continually remember. We'd sold our
Michigan summer house, giving much away, leaving behind
furniture as the buyers wanted it as furnished, turnkey. So,
after the sale, we simply drove away with what fit in our
Prius. Then, we decided to redo our Oregon home, downsizing as we went. Four dumpsters and more trips to the
local thrift store to donate than I can even recall, telling
ourselves we would replace "stuff" if needed. We looked
forward to house-hunting in the new season of life.

As Covid hit us both within a month, our future took
on a new look. Dan's new home turned out to be Heaven;

my new residence, moving to our son's home in Texas. And the affliction of dealing with grief, sadness, shock became my fog of reality. Our "new season" was not quite what I'd anticipated.

And yet there is hope, that little light that shines through the darkness of loss. Hope for what the Lord's new purpose is for my remaining years. Because of His faithful love, His comfort has sustained me in dimmest moments, so I know I can trust Him to open doors and opportunities. This hope, I'm finding, displaces all the frustrations and fears as they arise, threatening me with their storm of doubt that life will ever again have joy. As for the waves of grief that would toss me about, I can speak the Word to them: Psalm 46:10 "Be still and know that I am God. I will be exalted among the nations, I will be exalted in the earth." And He will! He will be exalted over the feelings, the self-pity, the inner-storms, and misgivings! Psalm 28:7 says, "The Lord is my strength and my (impenetrable) shield; my heart trusts (with unwavering confidence) in Him, and I am helped…" (Amp) There is nothing like the Sovereign, faithful, all-knowing, all-seeing, unchangeable strength of our Heavenly Father! He is my impenetrable shield! Nothing can get through to me, so my heart can trust, full-on rely, depend on Him with "unwavering confidence"!

It's truly because of the Lord's faithful love that I didn't and don't perish. I reread John 3:16, "That whosoever believes in Him shall not perish…" Do I recall the pain and poison of grief as my heart and body reacted to loss? Absolutely. But the Lord has sustained me. He provided in the past and will continue to provide in this new season. I know because His mercies never end.

Lord, May I never forget your unending faithful mercies. Thank You for light and leading along this new path before me, and for your faithful kindness. In Jesus' Name, Amen.

> **Grief notes: God is at work rebuilding our lives. Things that used to seem important fall by the wayside. I've seen what it means to gut a house and do a full-scale remodel. Redoing our lives during this time is the chance to rebuild with better character qualities, installing right priorities, and putting God in His rightful place.**

Journal 55

"He did not waver in unbelief at God's promise but was strengthened in his faith and gave glory to God, because he was fully convinced that what God had promised, He was able also to do." Romans 4: 20-21

Completely certain. Firmly believing. Confident. No doubts. Like Abraham who did not waver in unbelief at God's promise, I want to stay in that place of strength, where I am totally sure that God is able, no matter what. This is the rich ground of hope. This is also the ground of surrender. In being totally and fully convinced, I surrender, yielding my expectations of what I'd anticipated life's journey would be.

Yes, I'd naively anticipated life would go on decade after adventurous decade. Dan would sometimes say, "You'll need to know how to do this for someday when I'm not around." Me, rolling my eyes, I'd say something ridiculous. But then, loss, and he was gone. The early steps are wavering. Unsteady.

But I dove into God's Word, His promises. Knowing these: my Sovereign Father's promises of always being with me, of never leaving nor abandoning me, of an eternal home in Heaven, His forgiveness, the comforting counsel of the indwelling Holy Spirit. And prayer. Sometimes not my words, but Psalms became my heart response. Psalm 16: 5 became a constant: "Lord, You are my portion and my cup of blessing; You hold my future."

Abraham had no hesitation, no episodes of second-guessing in stepping out to follow God's request and it empowered his faith. He gave God glory because he was completely persuaded that God would do everything He had promised to do.

So, even in the middle of painful loss, I came to recognize that this is God's plan. I have God's Word on it in His promises. I am fully convinced that He can carry out His promises, and it will empower my faith as I give Him all the glory for His sovereign ways. His thoughts and plans are so far above anything I could ever imagine. I'm also fully convinced that He will "keep that which I've committed unto Him against that day." (1 Timothy 1:12 KJV)

Lord, Thank You for your promises to be with me, and the example of Abraham being firm in his faith in You, and the way You empowered his faith as he believed and stepped out in complete trust in You. Because Your promises will never fail, I can step out on the solid ground of faith as You lead me into this new season and a new purpose. May I continue to walk with this unwavering faith, surrendered to You. In Jesus' Name, Amen

Grief notes: Grief is a teacher. We learn how strong our faith is, and if we really believe God is who He says He is! We learn how precious life is and how important it is to prepare for death. We learn how important family is and to treasure our friendships.

Journal 56

"I am weary from grief; strengthen me through Your word." Psalm 119: 28

Grief is hard work. Don't let anyone tell you differently! And it's not just a series of "stages" or levels one must pass through to be "healed". Not even close. Did you ever cast a level wind fishing reel and get a backlash? Yes. Like that. With no reference point of where to start unraveling, it is fog, and chest ache, and then there's life business that needs attention. When mail that arrives in his name, and just seeing his name on the envelope slices like a knife. Then days will trail out, a sort of calm, and I think it's getting better, but then a song in a store will set you off again. Or just shopping and noticing the ice cream he'd buy for me. So wearying, these unpredictable burdens of memories hanging on me.

But then I realize this: I need to surround myself with what will strengthen me. I need to surround myself with what God says about my heart, my life now, my hope, and my comfort. Dan is currently surrounded by God's grace and His glory. So, I needed to feather my heart-nest with the promises that will help me now! There is only one way to get that strength from His word into my life! I must feast on it! My hunger for more of how His Word provides for my needs creates an appetite for these verses!

"In the day when I cried out, You answered me, and made me bold with strength in my soul." Psalm 138:3

"I can do all things through Christ who strengthens me." Philippians 4:13

"Let the words of my mouth and the meditation of my heart be acceptable in Your sight, O My strength and my Redeemer." Psalm 19:14

"My flesh and my heart may fail, but God is the strength of my heart and my portion forever." Psalm 73:26

"He gives power to the weak, and to those who have no might He increases strength…

But those who wait on the Lord shall renew their strength..." Isaiah 40: 29, 31

"Now to Him who is able to do exceedingly abundantly above all that we ask or think, according to the power that works in us..." Ephesians 3:20

"The eternal God is your refuge, and underneath are the everlasting arms..." Deuteronomy 33:27

Drawing help from His Word, I have a respite from the weariness of grief's relentless pull. These promises of help from God don't fail. And like His mercies, they are promised to be new every morning, for every new demand and that is how I am strengthened by His Word every time.

Lord, Your Word empowers me for the path You've chosen for me. I know I'll need these promises tomorrow, and the next tomorrow, as I lean in, trusting You, because You never leave, You never fail. Keep my lens of faith on the peace you provide in Your gracious strength. In Jesus' Name, Amen.

Grief notes: Grief can rob us of power, so we feel less able to cope with life. However, we have power because Christ arose from the dead. The apostle Paul said, "That I may know Him and the power of His resurrection" (Philippians 3:10). That same power is available to us as we step out in faith and hold onto what He has for us.

Journal 57

"You rejoice in this, even though now for a short time, if necessary, you suffer grief in various trials so that the proven character of your faith—more valuable than gold which, though perishable, is refined by fire—may result in praise, glory, and honor at the revelation of Jesus Christ." 1 Peter 1:6-7

I'm no carpenter, but I learned enough about building from my wise and talented remodeler husband to know that it's hard work. Building character is even harder. Even more so is the proven character of our faith. Paul confirms it's more valuable than gold that's been refined in the crucible. The fire of grief certainly refines our faith and builds faith's character as I rely on Christ for every need, strength, victory, and ounce of peace.

Because God is our living hope, we have an imperishable inheritance kept for us in Heaven (v.3-4). That's why we can rejoice even though we have these crucible times of grieving because it then that the fire burns away the dross and impurities of this life, revealing what matters most in life: Jesus and the better purpose for which we live, serving Him.

What is the result of all this refining process? It is the proven character, the tested, tried, and true quality of my faith that may result in God's praise, honor, and glory one day at the Revelation of Jesus Christ. After all, He is the One worthy. He is the One who has carried the load, provided the way, shown Himself to be Truth, and brought eternal life to the table. I mean, where would I be without Him? From minute one of this grief journey, His presence has kept me, although the purifying fires melted every part of my heart, the raging pain, seeming to fuse time and memory. And still the flames lick the dross, and I am still a work in progress.

This process humbles me. The very One who has been my strength, could I bring Him praise? In this reshaping of my life, can there be a new purpose here? Yes, there is new value along this path the Lord has called me to, this genuineness of faith that's being tested. I know it's more valuable than gold that will tarnish, wear out and perish. Even if now, for a short time, I suffer through this sadness, compared to eternity, any length of grief I'm sure will seem brief. So, Paul says to rejoice because God's power is guarding you! (v.5)

Even in suffering, and grief is one way we do suffer, we can trust in His process and His plan! He is doing this because rebuilding my character of faith is underway.

Lord, I trust You in this refining process of loss. I know You are rebuilding me in ways I may not understand, but I know enough of who You are to understand that I can put everything into Your faithful, loving hands. Help me with these steps of faith and character building. In Jesus' Name, Amen

> **Grief notes: Forgiving others is important during grief. The offhand comment may not have been intended to sting, but it did. Ask for grace when this happens, because unforgiveness opens the door for the Enemy to make life miserable (Matthew 18: 23-35).**

Journal 58

"Do not be conformed to this age, but be transformed by the renewing of your mind, so that you may discern what is the good, pleasing, and perfect will of God."
Romans 12:2

I remember when I had to start thinking like a married gal, and then when our boys came along, to start thinking of myself as a parent. Retirement was another one of those changes in thinking, as was becoming a grandparent. Life changes signal alterations in how we think of going about our lives.

There are so many ways the world attempts to step in and mold my thinking about my body image, what's trendy or a political agenda. The enemy also brings a barrage of shame reminders, dredging up past mistakes and regrets that I've already turned over to Christ. Discouragement and distraction are his timeless, well-worn traps to steal my focus and skew my thoughts. He enjoys reminding us of our past that no longer defines us because of Christ.

Now as I consider this new season, there is yet another way of thinking who I am: I am a widow, solo, no longer married. And I remember that I am not alone, for the His promised presence brings me peace and security, as well as calm to each storm as it rises.

The enemy does not want me to remember my blessings in Christ! More than ever, I need to home in on the key truth in this verse: "Don't be conformed to (formed with) this age but be transformed (changed) by the renewing of your mind." What do I really need? A new way of thinking! Not conforming to the world's idea of wisdom for a loss of spouse. Not being sucked into the bog of helpless, hopeless self-pity. Instead, I am to nab all those selfish, stray thoughts because "We demolish arguments and every pretension that sets itself up against the knowledge of God, and we take captive every thought to make it obedient to Christ." (2 Corinthians 10:5 NIV) Yes, I must push away the Enemy's lies of "You can't live without him in your life!" or "Life will never be good again!" The father of lies will try, but the victory to overcome that thinking is in Christ!

And that's how we can learn to determine or discern what is the good, pleasing, perfect will of God! What does God want me to do in this new season of life? Where is He leading me to serve Him? With a renewed mind, focused on Him, what new way of thinking awaits where He leads? As I lay those thoughts before Him daily, I'm know He can guard and change my thinking for what honors Him even in this time of loss.

Lord, renew my mind to focus on Your good, pleasing, perfect will that You have for me along this new journey. May I daily be transformed to be more of who You want me to be so I can discern the path you have laid out for me. In Jesus Name, Amen.

> **Grief notes: Sights, sounds, and smells can trigger re-experiencing the loss of our beloved. When that happens, remind yourself where you are now. Tell yourself that God has been faithful in the time since those events took place. You might send up a flash prayer of "Help, Lord." And He will.**

Journal 59

"Those who know Your name trust in You
because You have not abandoned those who
seek You, Lord." Psalm 9:10

The many names of God in scripture reveal His character, letting us know we can fully trust and rely on Him, implicitly, and recognize above all that He is Sovereign. Studying these is a faith game-changer! When you know who God truly is, we view Him differently. We can see all His qualities that show how readily we should place every circumstance and concern into His mighty capable hands.

Consider that He is:

Yahweh—The Lord, God (Deuteronomy 6:4)
Adonai—Master (1Samuel 24:8)
Elohim—Creator (Genesis 1:1)
Abba—Father (Romans 8:15)
Jehovah Jireh—The Lord will provide (Genesis 22:14)
Jehovah Rapha—The God Who Heals (Exodus 15:26)

Jehovah Nissi—This Lord is my Banner -declaration of protection (Exodus 17:15)

Jehovah Shalom—The Lord is Peace (Judges 6:24)

Jehovah Tsidkenu—The Lord our Righteousness (Jeremiah 23:6)

Jehovah Raah—The Lord is my Shepherd (Psalm 23:1)

El Roi—The God Who sees me (Genesis 16:13)

El Shaddai—The God Almighty (Genesis 17:1)

El Elyon—God Most High (Psalm 57:2)

When we begin to learn Who He is and to know His name, we can seek Him in full assurance and confidence that He will not abandon us and that He is faithful.

What a comfort this is to realize that He will provide and heal. To be secure in knowing He is my banner, my protection, and my peace. He sees me. In fact, He sees me seeking Him for He knows my needs even before I ask. His presence is with me as it was when He went before the Children of Israel. He was in all their tomorrows as well as the present, in the same way He will be in my tomorrows before I arrive.

The Word reveals so much of who God is and helps us to realize how much He loves us as well as how He provided saving grace through His only Son. How couldn't I put my full weight of trust in His ways? Why wouldn't I? I John 4:

16 reminds me: "God is love." Yes, He is the very embodiment of love. He is unconditional, unchangeable, unending Love, and so much more.

Lord, Your names teach me so much about You—Father, Creator, Provider, Healer, Protector, Shepherd, Peace, Love. Thank You that I can trust every step of this widow experience to You. May I remember daily to yield to Your hand on my life and my heart. I know Your lovingkindness and Your presence will never leave me. In Jesus' Name, Amen.

> **Grief notes: Self-talk is important in the grieving process. Remember that you can counter negative thoughts with promises from God's Word when you feel you are sliding into a sad state of mind. Remind yourself of times when you felt His presence, a prayer was answered, or even read aloud Psalm 23.**

Journal 60

"If you keep silent at this time, relief and
deliverance will come to the Jewish people
from another place, but you and your father's
family will be destroyed. Who knows, perhaps you have come to your royal position
for such a time as this." Esther 4:14

For such a time as this. This phrase has been echoing in
my heart and mind the last few days. Could this new path of
widowhood be a "royal position" in my life, at this moment?
Are there those in need of relief and deliverance I may be
able to reach by not staying silent about grace, strength,
comfort found in my Lord and Savior, Jesus?

If I keep silent. If I keep locked inside my grief, staying
in solitude with my sadness, I may miss the chance to bring
the message of the true source of comfort to someone who
doesn't know Christ yet. How else will they know the God
of all comfort Who has stood by me since I lost Dan? 2
Corinthians 1:3-4 reminds me that I was comforted so I

could pass along this source of comfort to others. I need to be a pass along this comfort and not keep it to myself.

Relief and deliverance will come. Yes, people will discover ways to cope with loss, but is it a manner that will heal and help long term? Some folks will turn to trying to reach their lost loved one through a medium to find ease from their pain of loss. We know well that God does not want us consulting with those dark arts of the Enemy himself. Others will turn to "things" that might fill the void for a time, but offer no real healing, often complicating their situation even more. No, the real answer lies in turning our pain, our questions, our need for healing over to the Master: The Lord. He has promised His comfort and His hope for the future. Remember that Proverbs 3:5 says, "Trust in the Lord with all your heart; do not depend on your own understanding." Real relief from the pain and ache of loss comes from the One Who can deliver us, bringing us to understanding that His ways are High and Holy.

"Who knows, perhaps you have come to your royal position for such a time as this." Esther's rise to the station of Queen was no coincidence. It was a divine appointment at a critical time: her people needed help as their very lives were at stake. Becoming a widow was not a mistake. God knew long before. I know Covid has taken many lives and brought grief and loss around the world, but many widows don't know Jesus. Or maybe they knew Him but have wandered so far away they don't feel there's still hope. Well, there is. God sent His Son to be the Savior of the world for whosoever believes in Him. I can ask the Lord to lead me to share His hope with someone who needs Him and His comforting today!

Lord, May I recognize those around me in need of hearing your good news today. Lead me to them and help me share the hope that is within me, this salvation and hope through Your Son. In Jesus' Name, Amen.

> **Grief notes: Sometimes we must make a choice and make a change. We often want to stubbornly hold on to the old days, but we must choose daily to take up our cross and follow Him, wherever He leads.**

Journal 61

"Pay careful attention, then, how you live—
not as unwise people but as wise—making
the most of the time, because the days are
evil." Ephesians 5:15-16

Sometimes grieving makes me self-focused. I tend to pull in and protect myself from triggers and ambushes, withdrawing to my own space when the waves hit me. I must remember that the Enemy is shameless, and he doesn't skip an opportunity to trip me up, grieving or not. So, Christ is calling me out of my personal reveries to remember all the Lord has done for me in the past, as well as all He's done strengthening me in this time of losing Dan, and all He promises for the future. I must live in a wise way and make my days count for God's purposes.

This future that God is walking me into is His new plan for me. So, I need to pay close attention to how I live. Am I living God's priorities for me? Do I seek His wisdom daily? Am I asking for His direction for the day? Am I absorbing the Word into heart and mind, so it is with me when I need it for direction or encouragement? Am I asking Him to bring my path across someone else's who needs Jesus? Am I listening for the nudge of the Holy Spirit to speak up, follow through, and bless someone I encounter? Yes, I need to pay attention, not being so self-absorbed, but absorbing the Word, making me ready for where He wants to use me in this new transition.

"Not as unwise people, but as wise, making the most of the time, because the days are evil." No, taking time to grieve and work on my grief process is not unwise; it's part of healing. By staying in my room, refusing to interact with others, now that begins to be unwise. My husband has moved on to his Heavenly home, but I am still here. In fact, my days to live for and serve the Lord are limited, too! He knows exactly how many days remain for me to live and work for His plan!

And make no mistake: the days are evil! More than ever people need to hear about how much God loves them, they need to hear that Jesus paid the penalty for their sin, and that there's a home in Heaven they have access to because of Jesus' sacrifice for them! Most importantly, others who mourn need to know there is a God waiting to bring hope and comfort to them, as well. Isaiah 6:8 says, "Then I heard the voice of the Lord saying, 'Whom shall I send? And who will go for us? And I said, 'Here am I. Send me." May I be ready when God asks that question of me!

So, "Pay careful attention" I remind myself. Time is precious. Like living currency, I dare not waste my time. I need to make the most of my days for the Lord, spending my moments wisely for the Lord's use, for His purpose.

Lord, May I always be attentive to opportunities to speak of You and the hope that is in You. May I continue to make the most of the time You have given to me for Your purposes. Make me ready to serve as well as willing to speak. May I hide Your Word in my heart, so it is available to win others for You. In Jesus' Name, Amen.

> **Grief notes: While we might be wrapped up in our own grieving, remember the rest of the immediate family, siblings and friends are grieving as well. Everyone grieves differently, so we need to be sensitive to how they are doing, too. Again, give grace to those who might be experiencing some of the aspects of grief we recognize like anger, guilt, and remorse. Pray that God would give you help in comforting them, as well.**

Journal 62

"But thanks be to God, who gives us the victory through our Lord Jesus Christ! Therefore, my dear brothers and sisters, be steadfast, immovable, always excelling in the Lord's work, because you know that your labor in the Lord is not in vain." 1 Corinthians 15:57-58

Yes, the enemy likes nothing better than to waylay my feelings, distracting and discouraging my thinking. He is just that menacing to me in this first year of my grief. But I have help, rather, I have a Helper! The Lord is with me! The Holy Spirit is my Comforter, my Counselor, and will direct me toward truth! In Him I have victory over whatever the Enemy tosses my way.

I'm realizing that the triumph of Jesus at the cross and His resurrection presents an entirely new kind of victory for me. Beyond the sin issue, Christ's victory means victory over my emotions and feelings that vacillate and sway and sometimes nearly sink me. Looking back in regret, looking around at loneliness, when I can sense the grip of fickle emotions on me, I know I am not walking in victory over what threatens to sink me. The Lord said that when the Holy Spirit would come, He would remind us of what Jesus had said! How about John 14:1, "Don't let your heart be troubled. Believe in God…" and verse 27, "Peace I leave with you. My peace I give to you." In John 1 :4 He says, "Remain (Abide) in me, and I in you." Again, I'm seeing John 8:32, "You will know the truth, and the truth will set you free." Then there is the promise in John 7: 38, "The one who believes in me, as the scripture has said, will have streams of living water flow from deep within him." The guarantee in Matthew 28:20 encourages me: "And remember, I am with you always, to the end of the age." So many ways the words of the Lord Jesus speak to us about living in victory as well as His peace, His constant abiding, His truth, His calming presence, and the flow of living water deep within that satisfies our soul's thirst for better days. And there can be better days right now. These are winning words to an emotion-prone heart.

I am so thankful I can turn to Him in my weakness and sorrow. It gives me hope to know that I am not alone, His purpose isn't yet complete for me, and that His promises are reliable and true. And best of all, His Spirit abides within me to remind me that no matter how bogged down I may get in my feelings, He is there with the truth. The truth of who I am in Christ; the truth of how I can know peace; the truth of how He is with me always.

That's why I can step out into God's new purpose for my new life with confidence, unwaveringly, knowing that what He's calling me to do won't be in vain. My triumph is only through the Lord Jesus.

Lord, I submit to you these emotions that sometimes run away with my imagination and impact my peace. I know your presence is a promise, as is your peace and rest. You have conquered the enemy who would distract with discouragement, fear, and despair. Your Holy Spirit points us to the truth, where those lies are broken. Thank You for the victory. In Jesus' Name, Amen

> **Grief notes: The path of grief toward healing is more like a rollercoaster. Some days, we feel like we are beginning to see progress, but the next day we may feel like tears win the day and we draw back. Remember, tears are healing. Let**

them fall, but through our tears we can read God's promises and thank Him for being with us. Eventually, there will be better days.

Journal 63

"Father if You are willing, take this cup away
   from me—-nevertheless, not my will, but
   Yours be done." Luke 22: 42

There at the foot of the Mount of Olives in the Olive
Grove of the Garden of Gethsemane, Jesus prayed. "Take
this cup if it be Your will." This was not the cup of blessing
they'd partaken of together at their last meal. No, this was
the cup of the curse. The cup of all the punishment for
sin and evil, as well as God's fury against it all. And Jesus
prayed on. In fact, He prayed so intensely to the point of
sweating blood. He knew what would lie beyond those
hours of agony and anguish of body and soul. However,
this was God's plan for us, for me, for all of us who have
come to believe.

So often since losing Dan, I've prayed in the anguish of
my heart. Searing and raw, those fresh, new hours of loss
seized my entire body. Shock waves were coursing through
me like I'll never forget. And in Jesus, I see how He can so

readily understand my measure of grief and loss. Yes, I know it was nothing like His Gethsemane or His Golgotha. But there's still so much for me to take away from this time that points me to His resolute, obedient, faithful heart.

"Father, if You are willing…" Jesus, as the Son, entreats His Father if He is willing to take away this cup. Is there another way? Is there another path that won't include the awful payment for barbaric acts against children? Another means what wouldn't include the punishment for war crimes, murder, abortion-on-demand, and abusive behaviors? Or another cup that wouldn't hold the untold evils of those who would never believe in Him anyway, so they'd serve the Enemy himself, twisting truth and leading others to follow their lies blindly? Even that cup for false followers who'd follow until it became inconvenient. No, Jesus took it all. Every drop that God the Father meted out for all sin. He knew it, and He still emptied that cup, becoming for us what should've been ours, so we could become righteous in Him. What a debt of love we owe Him.

Nevertheless. Still. Even so. Come what may. "Not My will, but Yours be done." Even Jesus stated this, knowing full well what His manner of execution would be, He surrendered to His Father in Heaven. He also knew the joy that was to follow: salvation for mankind. "For the joy set before Him He endured the cross, scorning its shame and sat down at the right hand of God." (Hebrews 12:2) "Your will be done." Just as He'd taught His disciples to pray: "Your kingdom come, Your will be done on earth as it is in Heaven." (Matthew 6:10)

It was not my will to have Dan pass into eternity on that day. But it was God's. I know Jesus understands the anguish of my loss and it has made it easier for me to say, "Your will be done," for He has a plan and a reason for this new life. I trust Him. He sees my future.

Lord, I submit myself to Your sovereign will for me today. May I be resolute and obedient to where You are leading me. I trust Your guiding and wisdom for this path. In Jesus' Name, Amen.

Grief notes: Sometimes we wonder if this loss is a punishment. No, it's not a punishment for anything we've done or didn't do. It is part of God's purpose and plan. He knows our last day before we live our first according to Psalm 139: 16. Someday we will understand, but for now we leave the mysteries with Him.

Journal 64

"So then, let those who suffer according to God's will entrust themselves to a faithful Creator while doing what is good." 1 Peter 4:19

I haven't the slightest doubt that God knows every bit of what I've suffered through this time of grief. Is it according to His will? Absolutely. He already knows how I will deal with this drastic change in my life. How will others view how I handle this sad loss? Will they see my turning to the Lord? So, what now? I'll admit I've had quite a few wobbly days when nothing seems clear. Habakkuk 3:19 says, "…My Lord is my strength; He makes my feet like those of a deer and enables me to walk on mountain heights." This deer's feet in those high places were hitting scree and loose gravel. So where does my footing come from? Who will strengthen these weak ankles? How will this transition of widowhood progress?

There is only one way to look ahead. It's in the trusting. Committing. Entrusting, handing over myself and every need to my faithful Creator. I need to relinquish my idea of what life will be and believe that the almighty, sovereign Father knows what all of my tomorrows hold. In Lamentations 3:22-23 it says, "It is because of the Lord's lovingkindness that we are not consumed, because His (tender) compassions never fail. They are new every morning. Great and beyond measure is Your faithfulness." (Amp) New every morning! What a faithful Creator we have as He continues to create new ways to show His compassion for us. Every. Single. Day. Why? Because the challenges of every day are different. Monday's mercies look different than Thursday's mercies.

While I am recognizing the ache and sorrow of this loss, I will make a conscious decision in faith to trust, committing the day, the pathway, and myself to Him while I occupy myself with ways to do what is good and right. I need to seek the Lord's purpose for this day, to ask for His leading in serving Him, and to spend time in reading His word and praying and asking direction.

Yes, this suffering that God asks of widows is a holy asking, but it's one that He provides for with strength, comfort, peace, and wisdom. The pain of grief grips hard, but God's grace is a firmer grasp, a keeping hold on my heart, soul, and spirit.

He is, after all, the faithful Creator, creating the answers to our every asking, providing the grace I need for this moment.

Lord, I am again committing this time of suffering to You. I don't have the answers, but You do, and that gives me some peace knowing these things are all in Your control. Even though I sometimes bring concerns to You over and over, You still comfort and strengthen me and provide Your peace. Help me to hide more of Your Word in my heart so I can recall it when I need it. In Jesus' Name, Amen.

> **Grief notes: Our grief is starting to heal when we can begin to realize gratitude for the privilege of having shared life with our beloved. Thanking the Lord for all the ways He blessed us through the life we shared can help restore joy.**

Journal 65

"But the Lord is faithful; He will strengthen and guard you from the evil one." 2 Thessalonians 3:3

In the early days of grief, as the reality of my "new season" set in, I began to read about grief, and how does a Christian grieve. I was learning to lean in on the comfort of the Lord, to call on Him for strength and peace as the heavy waves of sadness seemed to shake me to the core. I was discovering my need to consume scripture, in particular the Psalms. In fact, I found great comfort in praying the Psalms as they were like salve to my soul. But what I did not encounter in the grieving books was the idea of the very real onslaught of the enemy on my freshly wounded heart. The doubts, fears, misgivings were real and brought new misery to my heart. So, I again turned to Ephesians 6 to renew my understanding of God's protection plan.

The Armor of God verses were familiar to me as I'd journaled about them a year ago. However, in my widow's fog of trying to work through loss, tasks at hand that all widows must tend to, and dealing with so much newness life was throwing at me, there were some new alerts going off on my dashboard. Keep my shield of Faith soaked in the water of the Word to extinguish those fiery darts of the enemy!! Remember that the belt of Truth is The Truth, Himself holding all this armor together. I recall the vital protection of the Breastplate of His Righteousness which is not any of my own self-righteous thinking! The key to my head's protection is the Helmet of Salvation, securely fastened when I'd placed my trust in Jesus! Knowing that the sword of the Spirit, the Word, is kept sharp and ready to use when verses are hidden in my heart to do battle with what the enemy staged an attack. And those shoes, the preparation of the Gospel of Peace, were helping me stand on the eternal salvation provided by Christ that puts me at peace with God! Those shoes are in fact cleated into the eternal promises of His Word.

Yes, I was figuring out how the brazen and cruel enemy would attack my thinking, my heart, my faith, attempting to replace Truth with his lies, and trying to see that I would not stand firm, but lose ground. I will remember I am already clad with this armor that God has supplied. Without a doubt, I am convinced that this is how a Christ follower can face grief.

Lord, As I daily take account of Your powerful armor, I submit all these protections to Your faithfulness. I rely on Your Word to guide and keep me this day. I'm thankful I am already a conqueror in You. In Jesus Name, Amen

Grief notes: Christians do grieve. Some will quote only part of 1 Thessalonians 4:13, "That you will not grieve…", but in fact, the rest of the verse reminds us we don't grieve like those who have no hope. We have an amazing hope in Christ! Paul is simply prefacing the next 5 verses that detail the why behind this precious hope.

Journal 66

"Therefore, since we have such a large cloud
of witnesses surrounding us, let is lay aside
every hindrance and the sin that so easily
ensnares us. Let us run with endurance the
race that lies before us, keeping our eyes on
Jesus, the source and perfecter of our faith."
Hebrews 12:1-2

When I see something lying on the floor in my way, I know
it's a tripping hazard, so I'll move to grab it before I forget and
possibly end up stumbling over it! This journey of widowhood
is no different. Often if I haven't rested enough, eaten right, or
am feeling lonely or anxious, thoughts of self-pity and worries
of a "false future" are like snares to trip me.

This is when I need to stop, and turn my face to Jesus,
to the Word. The power of prayer to settle an anxious heart,
and the strength of His grace as I read the scriptures, that's
what the 'Therefore' is there for! That's why, because we have
all those Hall of Faith heroes in the previous chapter 11 of

Hebrews: Abel, Enoch, Noah, Abraham, Isaac, Moses, Rahab, Gideon, David, Samuel and many more who all demonstrated endurance in their faith! They walked with strong trust and reliance on God by their faith, although their lives were often marked with sustained hardship and difficult trials. These were all witnesses to God's hand on their lives, His sovereign character, His faithful lovingkindness. This "cloud" of witnesses would remind us: Don't get tripped up by the enemy; go for it; stay strong and keep going. Keep your eyes on Jesus (our Source and Perfecter). He knew what the shame and brutality of the cross entailed, so He suffered the cruelty, giving up His life, then rising again, and is now seated with God the Father.

So, run. Lay aside the hindrances that delay or trip me. Run through the days when grief screams, You are alone. No, I'm not. Run when sadness burns your chest and numbs your arms because it's midnight, you're still awake, burdened with memories that ache. Run when it's hard to take the next lonely step remembering this, He's been there. He was despised, separated from His Father, in agony and anguish of heart, soul, and body. Still, He endured. And because He did, we have salvation.

Just keep focused on Jesus, I tell myself. The Lord knows how to guide, keep, and strengthen me. He's led millennia of witnesses by His power and mercy. And without a doubt, He's guided more than a few widows. He can keep my path, too.

Lord, May I continue to keep my eyes on You, my Source and Perfecter on this journey where there may be tripping hazards. Give strength for the endurance I need to continually trust You for the steps forward. In Jesus' Name, Amen.

Grief notes: Depression is often a part of grieving our loss. We isolate, draw back from attending church, and avoid friends. Part of this is normal for grief, but sometimes a doctor or a counselor can help us determine if this is grief or if there's more going on.

"Such is the confidence we have through Christ before God. It is not that we are competent in ourselves…, but our adequacy is from God… For if the ministry that brought condemnation had glory, the ministry that brings righteousness overflows with even more glory…Since then we have such a hope, we act with great boldness." 2 Corinthians 3:4,5, 9, 12

My pathway is under new navigation. I was always so glad that Dan liked to be the driver as unfamiliar roads didn't bother him; he liked adventure, and I felt very confident in his navigation skills! But that's all changed now. These verses come to mind: Philippians 4:13, "I can do all things through Christ who strengthens me." Galatians 2:20, "The life I now live in the body, I live by faith in the Son of God, who loved me and gave Himself for me." Drive new roads, even in the dark? Check. Wade through a mountain of income tax information to send off to the tax guy? Done. Hop on a new interstate freeway to find Sam's Club? Completed. Start attending a weeknight fellowship with a house full of strangers? Uh, ok, I guess. So, I went. Hot dish in hand.

"Such is the confidence we have through Christ before God. It's not that we are competent in ourselves…our adequacy is from God." So, by now I know this: it's not about me. On my own, I might not take up the challenge to drive on roads I'm not accustomed to taking. I might think: this step is too hard, too overwhelming, too complex. The confidence to step out and step up to the challenges is from God. My adequacy for the tasks ahead today, tomorrow, down the proverbial road, all comes from God. On my own, I can't; through Christ I can.

The amazing wisdom and foresight of God was to prepare us for His purpose and plan. Even with the amazing Mt. Sinai experience, the people forgot the glory of God, forgot to follow Him. But now the marvelous advent of God sending His Son to be the Savior of the world, this is overflowing generosity, grace, and glory. And because of the hope we have in Him, we can be bold—greatly bold—even when grief makes us feel less than courageous.

Because of Jesus, this pathway looks different. I can have hope. I can step out of the circle I would draw around myself, because my confidence is in Him.

Lord, When faced with new tasks and new scenarios, remind me that my confidence comes from You. Because of all You have planned the way for my path forward, I will trust You with the details. You designed me, so You alone know my hesitations, but I surrender them to You for Your strength, wisdom, and grace. In Jesus' Name, Amen

> **Grief notes: Grief can affect our health drastically. It was recommended to set up an appointment with my doctor to have my blood tested and do a general wellness checkup.**

Journal 68

"Rejoice in hope; be patient in affliction; be persistent in prayer." Romans 12:12

Be joyful in hope, be patient in trouble, be persistent in praying. It's like a three-point hitch for the grieving heart. How do I link up to what the Lord wants me to do?

First, I need to recognize joy is deep contentment. This isn't all the emotion of the moment that can change so quickly. Being joyful in hope is trusting what is faithfully and mercifully promised in His Word. Romans 5:2 says, "We have also obtained access through Him by faith into this grace in which we stand, and we rejoice in the hope of the glory of God." And again, in Romans 5:5 "Such hope (in God's promises) never disappoints us, because God's love has been abundantly poured out within our hearts through the Holy Spirit who was given to us." (Amp) How amazing it is to realize that I can access joy and hope through these promises! It's as if they were written just for me! I soak these into my soul, knowing this is where joy comes from.

Be patient in affliction. Especially in this new season of loss, I find I need to be patient with myself when faced with surges of grief. I know this tide will not destroy my peace, for God has promised to give me the peace that passes understanding. But I can trust He will comfort me, as He is the God of all comfort. It may be a bit bumpy, but He has promised His grace is sufficient because His strength is made perfect in my weakness. There's no doubt that grief makes me feel weak.

Be persistent in prayer. This is my lifeline, praying without ceasing. Taking my needs to Him is an around the clock reality. Although hindrances and hurdles will come, I can persevere in prayer with faith that God hears, that He is working, and He will answer in His unique way, in His sovereign time. Do I have to wait? Yes, I wait and, in the waiting, He is preparing me for tomorrow.

As the Lord leads me along this journey, I know that He is calling me to trust that He will fulfill His purpose in my life in this new season. Psalm 138:8 says, "The Lord will accomplish that which concerns me [my purpose!], Your (unwavering) lovingkindness, O Lord, endures forever—Do not abandon the works of Your own hands." (Amp) Through a deep abiding joy in all He has done to care for me, through patience for His timing, and persisting in prayer for direction, guiding, and wisdom, He will give purpose in this path.

Lord, May I find joy in the hope you have given, the contentment You provide. May I be patient in this pain and suffering, knowing You are near the broken hearted. And may I persist in prayer, waiting with patient faith for Your answers. In Jesus' Name, Amen

> **Grief notes: The path forward in grief is a choice. I can choose to huddle in my current sadness and complain how life has changed, or I can choose to trust God for the unknown ahead and all His Word and presence has to offer.**

Journal 69

"You Yourself have recorded my wanderings. Put my tears in a bottle. Are they not in Your book?" Psalm 56:8

I am startled at the tenderness of this Psalm and the compassion of our Lord that radiates from these words. No matter the suffering, pain, and grief I am experiencing, He can trace every restless moment, every pang of loss, and loneliness. My tossing and turning on sleepless nights, He has recorded it in His book. My aimless meandering thoughts along pathways of yesterday, He knows each turn of thought and memory and He's made note. When I don't know where to go or what to do next, He knows. When I've had a few "good" days, and then a new layer of grief exposes new "loss", He is aware. Nothing escapes His notice, for He's with me. He anticipates my needs before I can even think to ask. His Holy Spirit reads and responds to my broken spirit. What gentle kindness from the Almighty God.

Not only is He so attentive in recording my restlessness, but He also knows each tear that falls. The Psalmist says, "Put my tears in a bottle." He makes note not only of my wanderings, but bottles up my tears, too! Tears are precious and healing. Jesus knew the depth of grief as He stood outside the tomb of His friend Lazarus and He wept. He deeply felt the loss of Lazarus, but He also likely wept for the situation of this sin-shattered world. He would use that moment to demonstrate that He is the Resurrection, and that Life was in Him. He knew that the sting of death and grief of loss were facts of our lives we'd all face. He also knew Calvary lay ahead, and that would change everything.

And still the Sovereign God holds all our moments in His view. My wanderings in suffering and loss as well as my tears of sorrow, "Are they not in Your book?" Yes, these days of grief are all well-known to God. He knows them and in fact He knew when they would happen, from long ago. So, since He is also the God of all comfort, He, like no one else, knows my path from here onward, the way this journey will take.

The journey before me now is one without Dan, but God leads, as I know He is with me always just as He was with the two of us over the years together. Through times of suffering and grief, He knows each ache, tear, storm cloud, yet His promise stands firm: I am with you. He knows what is behind me, and before me. He's made an account of this, all my wanderings and my tears. He has a purpose for this turn in my life. It's in His book.

Lord, Your kindness and compassion bring comfort like nothing else. You know every pang of loss, you see every tear. And You are with me, providing strength and peace that I cannot even fathom. Help me to share this hope I have in You with others who don't have this assurance, so they, too, will know the hope in You. In Jesus' Name, Amen

Grief notes: Our bodies react to grief, so we need to move them. I didn't feel like going to a gym, but I began to walk the fence line of the horse pasture with my granddaughter. It was good for both of us!

Journal 70

"But as for you, be strong; don't give up, for
your work has a reward." 2 Chronicles 15:7

Never let it be doubted: grief is work. Hard work. You
might feel able to deal with your loss one day, and the next,
feel as if you cannot function, as you feel helpless, weepy,
and uncertain you can carry on. As not normal as this may
seem, it is normal. But there is hope. 1 Thessalonians 4:13
says, "We don't want you to be uninformed about those
who sleep in death, so that you do not grieve like the rest of
mankind, who have no hope." So, as the grief work begins,
or continues, we can be encouraged, like King Asa heard
from the prophet long ago:

"But as for you…" We all grieve differently. Some are
quite private with their tears and try to work through the
pain away from the company of even friends and relatives.
Others are quite demonstrative, taking to social media to
share their ups and downs. How ever we choose to grieve,
it's going to be similar to our personalities. Nevertheless, we

all grieve. No one can tell us how to grieve, how long to grieve, or what is the right way to grieve. It's how you grieve that is important. The man of God told the King not to focus on what was happening to other nations, but to focus on what God was calling them to do. It's like grieving because you are to grieve as you personally need to grieve.

"…be strong" It's tough to tell yourself to buck up when your world is falling apart, but this is a command. The man of God told Asa, (v.4) "but when they turned to God in their distress and sought Him, He was found of them." God doesn't tell us to "Be Strong" and then back away. No, He is with us! His strength is made perfect in our weakness! I may have to remind myself, "Be Strong" many times and I must remember this: He is with me, He will never forsake me, and I can call on Him in my (every!) time of need! I can be strong, because that strength is His almighty, infallible, faithful power, and it's mine, too!

"Don't give up." Even though the "I just can't" reel may be scrolling on replay in my head, He reminds me to stay the course. Stand firm. Roman soldiers, I understand, sometimes drove nails in the bottom of their shoes like cleats to stand their ground in battle because once down, the battle was over.

"Your work has a reward." The work that goes into grieving moves us closer to healing, joy, and to the purposes God has designed for us on this journey of being a widow. And as with

King Asa, (v. 15) "So the lord gave them rest on every side." As believers in Christ, we have the indwelling Holy Spirit to direct us and remind us to find ongoing strength in the Lord. As we take all these cares to Him, He will provide rest.

Lord, You tell us many times in scripture to "Be Strong". May I always remember that the strength comes from you. I must trust You for this, for You are with me as I walk through days that need Your grace that alone is sufficient and sustaining. In Jesus' Name, Amen.

> **Grief notes: As the days go by, we start to look into the future, and it can be uncomfortable to try and look too far ahead. When that happens, look through the lens of faith. If we look through the lens of loss, we will focus on what and who is absent. Looking through the lens of faith helps us see God is with us, and we don't have to face the future alone. He knows the future, we do not, so anything we'd conjecture would be a false one made of fears.**

Journal 71

"Don't worry about anything, but in everything with prayer and petition with thanksgiving, present your requests to God…"
Philippians 4:6

The dictionary defines worry as "giving way to anxiety or unease; allow one's mind to dwell on difficulty or
troubles". Giving way is to retreat, to withdraw, like giving
way to the enemy and yielding, backing down, or surrendering. During grief, there are so many times that apprehension and fear can complicate our days. Holidays do that,
especially those firsts without our husband. Anticipating the
day can be almost worse than the day itself! Remember that
anniversaries, birthdays, Christmas, New Year's Celebrations
all provide opportunities to worry or to trust.

"Don't worry about anything…" Facing a first holiday
season without Dan, the apprehension started weeks in
advance. I wondered if I would be consumed with remembering 40 plus years of Christmases. Would I rehearse

regrets or offer prayers of thankfulness for the privilege of so many holidays with this great guy? I decided: I would pray. I didn't want to cede the holiday to worry, my tears would honor the loss, but I knew I was pushing back on the waves of pain that might "sink my boat". I pressed into God's strength to sustain me, and He did.

Paul says: with prayers and petitions, the asking for, with thanksgiving we give our requests, our needs to God. I must remember that He is the One who knows my needs before I do, the One who created me. He is the One who goes before and beside me so, who else would know how to handle these hard days but Him? He understands the load of memories, for He was there with us as they were being made. I know His grace is bigger than all my needs. So, I can genuinely thank Him for the years gone by, but just as important are the years yet to come. What has He planned for me in this new season? He still has a purpose for me, as I am still here! And so, I make my requests to God. This widow path I don't know, but He does. What will tomorrow bring? What will yet be required of me? And again, worry and fear can cast a shadow over my path, but Paul reminds us, "Don't worry about anything." Anything. Living situation? Car issues? Finances? Family squabbles? He is Lord of all that.

I've come to realize how much our faithful Lord has led me through already. He's just waiting to hear from me, asking where He wants me to be, showing Him that I am putting my full weight of faith confidently in Him. Although this path is new territory for me, He knows it. I must remember Proverbs 3:5-6, "Trust in and rely confidently on the Lord with all your heart and do not rely on your own understanding. In your ways acknowledge and recognize Him, and He will make your paths straight and smooth [removing obstacles that block your way]." (Amp) This is a clear command to trust, and a promise of what He will do. So, when I start trying to rely on my own faulty understanding, I must recall I am making a choice to trust and turn it all over to the Lord, no retreating, only surrendering to His way.

Lord, You promise to make my paths straight when I place my trust in You with all my heart. Help me remember to carry my daily needs and concerns to You. Because of Your faithful loving kindness to me, I have strength for the challenges of this day for You will take care of fear. In Jesus' Name, Amen.

Grief notes: Grief is heavy. Seek out a selection from scripture that gives an uplifting, positive word to cheer a heavy heart. Reread notes from friends who've sent kind words to you by card, text, or email. It is true that "Kind words are like honey, sweet to the soul and healthy for the body." Proverbs 16:24. (NLT)

Journal 72

"For I am the Lord your God who holds
your right hand, who says to you 'Do not
fear, I will help you." Isaiah 41:13

Some days the flood gates open and I feel the storm of grief descend all over again. If I'm Hungry, Anxious or Angry, Lonely or Tired, I feel vulnerable to the rising tides of sadness. Someone came up with the acronym HALT for these stressors. And it's true as these are contributors to our feeling more depressive. When I'm tired and stressed, new challenges stick out their foot to trip me or I'm tempted to peer into the future where the enemy whispers "You can't do this." Oh. Yes. I. Can. Well, with the Lord I can! And "I can do all things through Him who strengthens me!" (Philippians 4:13) Besides, God is the One who can bring us through these times of distress.

In Isaiah 41:13, God Himself speaks to His people, "For I am the Lord Your God." The other nations boasted of their false-god idols, but they were of no help. This was the

Creator of Heaven and Earth speaking, Almighty, Sovereign, faithful, and kind. When I remember all that He has done for me, I know this is the One who can help me weather the waves and storms of grief. "For I am the Lord your God who holds your right hand…" The God of Heaven cares enough to hold my hand and lead me, as well as comfort me along the way. I don't have to stress over oil changes, bank changes, insurance changes, or my marital status change: the Lord Himself is with me, Emmanuel! God with us. That was Jesus! The Holy Spirit indwells the believer as our ever-present Helper! Our power to carry on day by day. God always cares for His people, even in their grieving. He's near to the broken-hearted. Even when I am tired, stressed, lonely, or have forgotten to eat!

"Who says to you, 'Do not fear, I will help you'." Yes, God says this as a command. In fact it's repeated many times in scripture! Do not fear! Even when life looks bleak and lonely? He tells me not to fear. He will help me. When it takes seven phone calls to straighten out a medical plan? Do not fear! He's got this, too. When I can't see the next step? Do not fear, He's been there, and He's with me. He knew this day from before I was born. His help is always present.

Thankfully, we can turn to our Lord for the help we need when fear and despair make it seem we are without assistance. The enemy wants me to panic, but God's direction is clear: Do not fear. So, instead, I can open God's Word and read promises and reminders of what a help He is to all who trust His leading. I can even read of how to ask for His wisdom in James! I can turn to Him in prayer, asking for strength and peace, when I feel weak and distressed.

Lord, Thank You for Your presence that dispels the darkness of fear with the light of Your promise and gives me hope. And I know that hope doesn't make us afraid because Your love is spread through our hearts. Help me to reach for this gift whenever I am feeling the distress of grief and loss. In Jesus' Name, Amen

Grief notes: Widow fog stays around for a while, so I began making a to-do list for the day. It helped organize me, helped me remember, and it brought a feeling of accomplishment when I could check off a task. I began to call it my brain!

Journal 73

"Set your minds and keep focused habitually on things above [the heavenly things], not on things of earth [which have only temporal value] …put on the new [spiritual] self who is being continually renewed in true knowledge in the image of Him who created the new self." Colossians 3:2, 10 (Amp)

Every day I set a goal to surrender my words and thoughts to the Lord. Sometimes it's many times during the day reminding and returning myself to where I should be "dwelling", seeking what is above, where Christ is. And for that matter, that's where Dan is, too. I tell myself that he is praising and rejoicing with the Lord, and so should I! And that's something we can do together. His Heaven's praise, and my earthbound praise. As I spend time focused on the Heavenly things, I can see that earth's "treasures" hold so little value by comparison. "For where your treasure is, there your heart will be also," Matthew 6:21 (NIV)

The things this world offers have only a temporary value. It reminds me of the stock market, up one day but it can dive low the next. Turning my thinking consistently to what is eternally important keeps a new reality before me. Eternity stands before every soul, every person I know, every clerk who waits on me at the store, every delivery person bringing my packages. That person I chat with casually at Walmart. The lady at the bank. The nurse who is taking my blood pressure. Every. Single. Person. This is knowledge I already knew on some level, but until Dan went to be with Jesus, it didn't have the urgency I now feel.

"Put on the new [spiritual] self who is being continually renewed in true knowledge in the image of Him who created the new self". This is our new spiritual self that is being continually renewed with true knowledge and discernment into the image and likeness of our Creator. Not only do we have new birth in Christ, but He begins the forming of a new character in us. This character is what God originally wanted us to be before sin stained the world's DNA.

Yes, the enemy would like to derail my thinking while I'm trying to set my thoughts on Heavenly things above. He'd like to distract me with fear, despair, and self-pity. He wants to encourage my "old self", yet God has other ideas. I'm finding that what the Lord began long ago in my life, now has new restructuring in this season called "widow". I am choosing to trust the Lord to lead me in this way He has for me, committing to putting less value on the temporary, focusing on the eternal perspective that is spiritual and that will continue to renew my character to be more like Him and to more readily share with others the hope I have in Him.

Lord, You call me out of the mindless things of this world to discover the ways You are renewing me to be more like Your image. I've become much more aware of the eternal, and I can see that the things of time hold little value except for how it's used for You. Help me to yield to your renewing, recreating hand on my life, and to serve You as I share your hope You've given me. In Jesus' Name, Amen

> **Grief notes: Grief is like a painting of your life that is completely washed in a new shade. All the details of your world are totally shaded with this hue. At first, that is all you see, although the original details can still be perceived. As time goes on, new details are added, but there is always that background shade visible. Grief indeed changes us and how we live going forward.**

"A great windstorm arose, and the waves were breaking over the boat, so that the boat was already swamped. He (Jesus) was in the stern, sleeping on the cushion. So they woke Him up and said to Him, "Teacher! Don't you care that we're going to die?" He got up, rebuked the wind, and said to the sea, "Silence! Be still!" The wind ceased, and there was a great calm." Mark 4: 37-39

Jesus knew the storm was coming before He and the disciples even entered the boat to cross the Sea of Galilee. He was also tired when He climbed aboard. The crowds had been demanding, and He had given. Now, Jesus fell asleep on a cushion in the back, allowing the veteran fishermen to face a sudden blasting storm that would shake them to the core.

It seems that the Sea of Galilee in Northern Israel is surrounded by hills, and it lies low in a valley with lowlands.

It is about eight miles wide, and twelve miles long. This body of water is situated such that brawling windstorms can suddenly occur, blowing violently in over the eastern hills, falling onto the lake.

Sudden storms are hard to deal with. We don't see them coming. Grief sometimes sneaks up on me, triggered by the unexpected, and I feel the boat start to shift beneath the gale force squalls and the rising swells of sadness. At once I'm reeling, and like the disciples, I'm asking where is Jesus now? Doesn't He know what's happening? I'm drowning here!

Yes, He knows. The all-knowing, all-seeing, faithful God knows. And I remember God's promise: "The Lord is the one who will go before you. He will be with you; He will not leave you or abandon you." (Deuteronomy 31:8) So yet again, I cry out to the Lord and yet again, He rebukes the sudden waves of sadness, reminding me to trust. He's reminding me that Dan is in Heaven where he's supposed to be now, and I am where the Lord has placed me.

"Silence! Be still!" The Lord's command still holds power today in my life. What rises up to defeat me is subject to my Jesus. His victory over sin, death, and the grave means the enemy may bring storms, but my Savior is in the boat. He knows the storms before they hit, and yet He waits for me to trust Him. I know when I ask, He speaks and those sudden winds will cease, and His calm will follow.

Lord, the storms of grief sweep in sometimes so abruptly, no warning, and I feel I'm right back at the beginning all over again. I am thankful that You are with me, and You know each approaching tempest, so help me to recall Your promises of being with me. Thank You for Your peace that passes understanding and for Your all-sufficient grace. I know I can trust in You totally during these stormy times. In Jesus' Name, Amen.

> **Grief notes:** The question always seems to come up in widows' circles: how long do I wear my wedding rings? Some remove them shortly after loss, while others are still wearing their rings a decade later. It is completely up to the individual. Nothing dictates one way or the other. Some have all of the rings, yours and his, refashioned into a pendant by a jeweler. Others place their rings on a chain to wear. However you choose to deal with your rings is right for you.

Journal 75

"Oh, Lord God! You Yourself made the
heavens and earth by Your great power and
with Your outstretched arm. Nothing is too
difficult for You." Jeremiah 32:17

When the fog of grief lifts a bit, I can look back in awe
over the past few months that seem like years and yet like
yesterday, all at the same time. I am beginning to appreciate
that the great Creator's power and outstretched hand has so
far done beyond all I could ever have imagined. Days and
weeks that have been so unbelievably hard, He has made a
way to bear, to find, or begin to find, a purpose in this pain.

When God allows, He creates a means, and it is always
for our growing closer to Him, more like Him, and more
able to reach others for Him so that from our story, we
can bring Him glory. Romans 5:3,4 says, "We can rejoice,
too, when we run into problems and trials, for we know
that they help us develop endurance. And endurance
develops strength of character, and character strengthens

our confident hope of salvation." (NLT) Rejoicing in my suffering was not my idea of the path that would lead me closer to God, or to sharing Jesus with others. The hurting made me recoil, the "not so close—I'm grieving" attitude gave me excuses to isolate, but God pointed out a few details to me: I was on thin ice, as the enemy was encouraging this attitude. He reminded me His grace was sufficient for me, His strength is made perfect in my weakness. Again, He prompted me to "Trust in the Lord with all my heart and do not rely on your own understanding." (Proverbs 3:5) I was realizing my understanding was subject to my feelings, and they were not reliable, especially right now. So, I trusted. Trusted like never before. Verses I'd known for decades suddenly came to life. Like Psalm 37:5 "Commit your way to the Lord; trust in Him, and He will act." And. He. Did.

"There is nothing too difficult for You." Our Creator is still creating. He creates hope where it seems least likely to appear. He creates joy even though grief is shaking my world. He's creating blessings where only He can make them grow. He's bringing prodigals home. He's opening doors and creating opportunities I've never seen before. And I can only say "Nothing is impossible for You, Lord." As I trace His footsteps of preparation over the previous years, I know now what I didn't realize then. And it builds my trust in Him even more. His plan, as Job said, cannot be thwarted.

Lord, Your faithful grace and strength in my weakness have increased my trust in You. I surrender (again) my needs to You, for Your ways are Sovereign. Thank You for Your Word that is helping me heal, as well as Your Holy Spirit who counsels and comforts through Your promises. In Jesus' Name. Amen

Grief notes: I recall visiting a California olive oil tasting room. The process of making olive oil reminds me of grief and suffering. Olive trees are shaken and often poles are used for beating the trees to remove the fruit. Finally, to make the olive oil, the fruit is crushed between stones or a mortar and pestle, and often heated, then pressed again between stones. Sometimes the crushing pain of loss seems unbearable, never-ending, but I recall what value the olive oil holds, and I remember God never wastes our pain. He will bring value out of suffering when we give it to Him.

Journal 76

"Do not despise these small beginnings, for
the Lord rejoices to see the work begin."
Zechariah 4:10 (NLT)

Small steps, humble beginnings were being made in
rebuilding the Lord's temple. Every heart who'd heard of
or remembered Solomon's beautiful original temple likely
felt the comparison. Yet the angel reminds Zechariah to
tell the king: "Not by strength or by might, but by my
Spirit, says the Lord of Armies." (V.6) This was going to be
a work of God.

Walking into this new year, I'm reminded that many
folks are making new resolutions for new diets, new exercise regimens, new ways of organizing their lives, but I'm
sitting here sizing up this new season of life: being a widow.
There are baby steps of surrendering all this newness to
the Lord: I'm in a new state (I moved 2,037 miles), new
living arrangement (staying with my son and family), new
church (amazing community, GriefShare classes), new roads

to learn (many at 75 mph!). These are all in addition to my new solo-ness as I navigate this new time of life.

I get tempted to compare. To compare my yesterdays with my todays. The "old season" with this new season. To relate what was my "comfort zone" with I'm now responsible for! These are small beginnings, I know. Taking small steps forward, walking with grief and trusting God. Leaning on His promises, staying in His word, praying for His wisdom, and guiding hand. All of these keep me committed to the structure of this new journey. Stepping out in faith, I believe there is yet a plan for my life that He will reveal.

"For the Lord rejoices to see the work begin." Although the beginning of rebuilding the temple was small, the foundation had been laid and this was a major commitment they made to complete what had begun! "And his hands will complete it," the Lord tells Zechariah. I trust that the Lord will complete His work and purpose in me, too. In verse 7, "What are you, great mountain? Before Zerubbabel (the king) you will become a plain." Now, that is some major hill-flattening! He will do it! Whatever that mountain is ahead of me, He can handle it. I just have to remember to trust Him and His timing, His Plan. I know His will be done because He always completes what He's begun.

So, I am realizing cannot compare what has been with where God is taking me in these days of new, small beginnings. He is working His plan in my life, a new season, a new purpose from this transition. I am taking baby steps and working toward the building and completion He has in mind.

Lord, Thank You for the foundation you are building in this new life. I know You will bring it to completion, so will not compare my "old season" to this "new season" You have called me to. Instead, I place this path ahead of me in Your hands. Lead, guide, and direct my days as I lean in on Your promises. In Jesus' Name, Amen.

Grief notes: Looking with new eyes on the story of Gideon, I notice how God works in unique ways. The handful of men geared up for battle with the Midians, taking trumpets and pitchers that contained torches. At a signal, they blew trumpets, broke the pitchers and the torches flared as the enemy ran. When we are broken, our light shines through and it becomes evident where our power comes from.

Journal 77

"Oh, the joys of those who…delight in the
law of the Lord, meditating on it day and
night. They are like trees planted along the
riverbank, bearing fruit each season. Their
leaves never wither, and they prosper in all
they do." Psalm 1:1-3

I had been writing scripture journals for a few years,
making it a daily habit to center my writing around one
verse that spoke to me, a topic that drew me, or a compel-
ling story I wanted to dig into. My time reading and writing
brought me joy to learn more of God's word in this way,
making me mine deeper into scripture, digging for treasure.
After Dan passed away, when reading scripture became a
lifeline for my heart and soul, no less than my survival, I
began to journal about those comforting passages that the
Spirit brought to my attention. Finding His comfort, peace,
wisdom, and grace in the searing agony of those early days
when the pain seemed unbearable, His Word was a salve.

Because I had already made it a habit, it was a natural fit to move into finding and "storing" these gems of promises that He provided. "Meditating on it day and night" was what calmed my soul and brought perspective to my new situation.

"They are like trees planted along the riverbank…" So, I began to appreciate the life of the tree planted near a river: fresh water, flowing through my heart and soul. Fresher still because I'd never read these words as a widow. Psalms that were my heart cries, I prayed these over and over. This refreshing water has an eternal source that we have no fear of its ending; Jesus says in John 4:14, "…the water I will give him will become in him a well of water springing up to eternal life."

And then I read this: "…bearing fruit in each season." How could I bear fruit in this season?! My helper, my partner-in-life is now gone! Are widows fruitful? The verse says—-in each season! What now does the Lord have for me to do, my new assignment in this new season? Philippians 4:13 reminds me "For I can do everything through Christ, who gives me strength." That made the possibilities wide open!

"Their leaves never wither, and they prosper in all they do." As I begin spending time in God's Word, I was finding there a delight (Yes, delight. I'd never read these passages with a widow's perspective!), soul strengthening, and mind refreshing. I could see that focusing on these scriptures would keep me spiritually healthy as I begin this transition, offering me hope on those days that might not seem so hope-filled.

And "Oh the joys of those" who do. There's the purpose: Joy. Planting and growing that joy that seems so elusive in grief and loss, yet knowing it is only found in the Lord, who is my only source of strength.

Lord, As I spend precious time with You, reading and meditating on who You are, I'm humbled and thankful for all You have done. May I continue to drink the water of Your Word that refreshes my faith and restores joy. In Jesus' Name, Amen.

> **Grief notes: Life will not be "normal" again for us. That frustrates some folks who want us to be on a path to "getting back to normal". There will be a new normal that develops over time, as we begin to heal, but we will not return to our "old" selves. Be kind to yourself as this realization becomes clear and be forgiving with any who struggle with your new self. Give them God's grace.**

Journal 78

"…we do not give up. Even though our outer person is being destroyed, our inner person is being renewed day by day." 2 Corinthians 4:16

We do not give up, I remind myself. Others have walked this journey. This place is not unique to me. It is new to me, but the Lord will lead me as He's led others.

Our outer person, so visible to the rest of this sin-stricken world, is in a downward spiral. Age, stress, grief all takes their toll on these bodies. So many physical effects of grieving leave us with sleepless nights, higher blood pressure, hair loss, and less-than-optimum bloodwork.

And yet there is hope for our inner person. The ache of loss finds solace in the God of all comfort. The anguish of loneliness finds hope in the One who is our living hope and finds a way to continue, day by day. The broken-hearted and crushed in spirit finds the nearness of God saving and strengthening them. Renewing, reshaping, repurposing, the

Lord begins a new work in us. He renews and regenerates what seems so unfixable, making a way where there seems to be no way. He reshapes what we cannot imagine, as the potter remakes the clay that collapses and begins anew to create a different vessel under the pressure of His wise hands. He repurposes our lives, giving us a new purpose in a new season, preparing us for a new area of service.

Day by day. God led the Children of Israel step by step. There was a pillar of cloud, step by step. At night, there was a pillar of fire, step by step. And so, day by day, God is working. Daily bread yields daily strength. "Do not fear, for I am with you…I will strengthen you…" (Isaiah 41:10). And so I find His daily steadfast love. "For the Lord will send His faithful love by day…" (Psalm 42:8).

This is why I do not give up or give in to despair, discouragement, or darkness. The Lord is renewing my inner person for this new season, this new journey. I take a step, His light on my path will reveal the next footfall. Although at times it might seem easier to give up and give in to the surge of gloom and life's-never-going-to-be-good-again, I know He's working on my inner person. He's making me stronger, making me more reliant on His strength. I know that's how His Spirit reinforces my spirit with the groans that only He understands. In the daily renewal of my trust in Him I am experiencing the reality of His peace and calm.

He's at work in me, day by day renewing and rebuilding a new life of purpose and service. When the Enemy murmurs "You can't", the Spirit whispers, "Don't give up."

Lord, Your love and grace surround me. Your ways of dealing with my grief are reliable and without fail. You love me so much; you continue to heal and renew me in my innermost person. Your Spirit is at work in me, in places where peace and joy can take root again. Direct my steps to follow You closer along this new path day by day. In Jesus' Name, Amen.

> **Grief notes: As He fasted in the wilderness, Jesus was tempted by the Enemy at His hungriest, yet He responded with scripture, the Word of God. Our truest source of defense from the doubts, fears, and misgivings the Enemy throws our way at our weakest is by speaking God's promises.**

Journal 79

"But the Lord stood at my side and gave me strength." 2 Timothy 4:1

Weakness, sadness, fear, and loneliness are frequent company for widows. Many times, and in many ways, these visitors crept in as if to stay. They seemed so sincere in assuring me they'd stay close to all those who are grief-stricken. As if they alone would see me through, framing each memory, magnifying my past like it was everything, and cautioning me not to plan for a future. They seemed like Job's miserable comforters.

Friends and family were good at offering comfort and support in the cards, letters and flowers that lifted my spirits. These were loved ones who knew us, loved us, and cared about the anguish I was trying to come to grips with. But in time, life calls them to carry on with their world of pressing needs. They could not keep up that level of tending to me, checking on me, reassuring me. I had to be realistic: they had their lives to live.

And so did I. But how would this new life look? Where was I garnering the strength to make it day by day? Evening by lonely evening when the sun would cast shadows on the walls, and I would realize: another day has passed, and there's no one here to process the day with, to plan for tomorrow with, or to even do a mindless crossword puzzle with!

"But the Lord stood at my side and gave me strength." As I began to call on Him, reminding Him that I am weak, He gave me the strength to face the hours that hung heavy. His Word gave me promises of His daily new mercies, His abiding presence: He would never leave me nor abandon me. His Word also reminded me to "Be Strong" because He was my strength! I had to trust Him like never before. I had to trust Him like the Israelites stepping into the Jordan River, walking by faith into the Promised Land. They stepped off the banks into that riverbed, following the command to GO. It was all new territory: "…for you haven't traveled this way before." (Joshua 3:4) I am starting on this new journey, as they did, and trusting that He will lead my steps forward. I, too, have never traveled this way before.

I know the Lord has a plan for the days ahead where He will guide me. I also trust that He will stand by my side no matter the challenges, for He is the Champion of Widows, and His grace will be sufficient. He knows I've never been here before, but I'm learning that I can trust what is ahead to Him. He will strengthen me, preparing me for the terrain before me, for His strength is made perfect in my weakness, sadness, loneliness, and fear. I am making the choice to trust whatever lies ahead into His faithful, gracious, capable, almighty hands.

Lord, You stand by me and strengthen me for the journey You have called me to. Challenges may take me by surprise, but they are no surprise to You. You have seen the way I will travel, so I submit my every need to You. I know that You will always guide and comfort me when I call on You. In Jesus' Name, Amen.

Grief notes: For Christians, we know where the soul and spirit of our loved ones are when they pass away. The Bible says a lot about the wonderful place that Jesus is preparing for us, with no tears, no suffering, and no more death. We are assured that upon death, we are absent from the body, and present with the Lord.

Journal 80

"'Though the mountains move, and the hills shake, my love will not be removed from you and my covenant of peace will not be shaken,' says your compassionate Lord." Isaiah 54:10

The mountains have indeed moved, and the hills have shaken these past months. In fact, my life has been turned upside down in almost every aspect. Except for one. Knowing the One who is my source of peace and understanding the value of His promises, I know the shaking and upturned life is completely in the plan that's been in progress since before my birth. Because I am His child, covered by His covenant of blood, I don't need to fear the future. Where He's leading me through this time of loss is a mystery only to me.

"…my love will not be removed from you…" Surrendering, giving up this upheaval of grieving to Him provides me with the security I need when knees quake.

Stepping back, I can see how patiently and tenderly the Lord has led me through this dark valley. Through this widow's hazy thinking, the Lord has been near and His Word a light of hope. On the days my mind begins to clear, new realizations of loss dawn on me and add to a heavy heart. Yet He makes it so clear that He is right there, and I can confidence that He will bring help and peace to my war-torn mind. He alone knows what lies ahead and will not only shelter me but lead me to what He has in mind for me in the days and the years ahead. "God is our refuge and strength, a helper who is always found in times of troubles. Therefore, we will not be afraid, though the earth trembles and the mountains topple into the depths of the seas, though its water roars and foams and the mountains quake with its turmoil." (Psalm 46:1-3)

His love is the origin of my unfathomable peace, my shelter from the storm that is rocking my world. "And the peace of God, which surpasses all understanding, will guard your hearts and your minds in Christ Jesus." (Philippians 4:7) That covenant of peace that Jesus paid for on the cross is mine, is guarding my heart and my mind. When emotions, those untrustworthy agencies that try to dictate my day, sail in on a wistful breeze, demanding I color my thinking with an idea that God can't possibly handle this situation, I must stop and remember His strength, that His peace is available always, and His love is not changeable.

So, even though my life landscape may appear to be shaking, quaking, and not at all what I'd imagined it would be, God knew this day was coming long ago. And if He in sovereign love allowed these life changes, He can keep me in His constant lovingkindness and continual peace. 2 Timothy 2:12 says, "…for I know whom I have believed, and am persuaded that he is able to keep that which I have committed unto Him against that day." (KJV) He is more than able. Exceedingly, abundantly able, to do above all I could ever ask or think.

Lord, You know so well how this grief journey has caused mountains to move and hills to quake. And yet Your strength and grace has kept me, steadied me. I am so thankful I can surrender these times to You and Your unshakeable love and peace. Guide me into the path You have chosen for me. In Jesus' Name, Amen.

Grief notes: Many folks, trying to comfort us, will quote Romans 8:28—that all things work together for the good

of those who love God. This can feel offensive if we interpret it as God caused our loved one's death. In the weeks and months that follow fresh grief, we come to appreciate that God can bring good out of our loss and that He can bring purpose out of our pain.

Journal 81

"I call to God Most High, to God who fulfills
His purpose for me." Psalm 57:2

"The Lord will fulfill His purpose for me. Lord, Your faithful love endures forever." Psalm 138:8

In the quiet moments, questions swirl. What now? What is next? Reflecting over life, loss, and trying to get a picture of what stretches out before me now, I realize there's a choice I have to make every day. Honestly, I daily remind myself that Dan is no longer living. He's not out of town, not simply on a trip he'll return from. This is permanent. He's in Heaven. And most importantly: God will help me today. I know it sounds strange, but my brain needs that reminder. I need to start every morning choosing this fact: it's going to be God and me today. His Word lies open in front of me with my morning tea, and I listen for His voice as I read. I open my prayer journal and I jot down praises for how His answers have sustained me. I thank Him for His grace and provision. I present my needs, and concerns for family and friends. And I end with, "Your will be done." I'm learning. Learning to recognize His sovereign will has my best interest and is my best way going forward.

So, what now? "I call to God Most High." He alone is the all-knowing, all-seeing, almighty, Lord of Angel Armies. Who else is Higher than He is? Isaiah 55:9 says that His ways and thoughts are higher than ours. Calling out to the Lord in prayer has been a lifeline for me. I Peter 3:12 reassures me that "the eyes of the Lord are on the righteous and his ears are open to their prayer." No one knows me like He does, no one has traced the path of my life so far like He has, and no one knows what lies before me like He does.

"I call…to God who fulfills his purpose for me." Not only does He know what lies ahead, He is the Almighty God, the only One Who can fulfill His purpose for me, directing my way towards what He has already sovereignly ordained as His next area of service for me. He is the Shepherd; He renews my life; He leads me along the right paths for his name's sake. (Psalm 23:3) He's made it clear in the darkest valley, He's there with me and I find comfort in the fact that His defensive rod of protection and the staff of His guidance have reinforced my trust.

"The Lord will fulfill His purpose for me…" I can rely on the fact that He is faithful. If He has said He will do it, I can trust His promise to fulfill His plan and purpose for me. Why? Because His "faithful love endures forever." The Lord's eternal scope of planning and caring for me helps me realize how deeply I can trust Him. Psalm 136:1 reminds me "Give thanks to the Lord, for His is good; for His loving kindness (graciousness, mercy, compassion) endures forever." (Amp)

And what now? I am learning to lean on Him, wait on Him, and trust that He is going to fulfill His purpose in me. And I choose to trust He will do it.

Lord, I'm thankful for the promise that You will fulfill Your purpose for me. As I look to You and Your Word, open my eyes of faith to follow You. May I willingly walk with Your grace in the path where You lead, in the strength You provide. Thank You for being with me on this journey. In Jesus' Name, Amen.

Grief notes: Someone may try to comfort us with the words, "I understand" when they have never been a widow. They may have experienced loss but have never had the experience of losing a spouse and all that entails. Give them some grace and recognize that it is a blessing they have not experienced the knowledge of the pain you are suffering.

Journal 82

"Jesus answered him, 'What I am doing you
don't realize now, but afterward you will
understand.'" John 13:7

Make no mistake. One day our lament of why will
be answered. One day it will all make sense, this loss, these
hard days of struggling to understand. Meanwhile, I will
search the Word for promises of how afflictions produce
endurance, endurance creates proven character, and proven
character generates hope and afterward, we won't ever be disappointed with that hope, because that's where God's love
is poured out into our hearts by the Holy Spirit (Romans
5: 3-4). God knows what He is doing.

I am learning to trust that His sovereign plan is always
good and it is for the good of those who are called according
to His purpose (Romans 8:28). That is a steep learning
curve for an aching heart. But finding His strength where
His grace is sufficient for this step, this moment, can move
me through the minutes, hours, days, and finally weeks. In

that time lapse, I discover how good God has been, His comfort like a soothing salve, His faithful love holding me steady like an anchor as the layers of loss unfold. Afterward, I recognized that His grip is far greater than whatever would try to remove my hope.

Jesus had knelt humbly to wash His disciples' feet like a servant before that Passover meal. and Peter questions Him. Yes, Peter, like me, struggled with questions, asking, and answering them. So, the Lord replies that they will realize why later or "afterward". After He would be crucified. After Peter would deny knowing Him. After the resurrection, when He would appear to them as they hid behind locked doors. After the Ascension, when all the disciples would stand in awe watching Jesus Christ rise into the Heavens. And after Pentecost when Peter, now overflowing with faith from what he had witnessed of the Resurrection, and the powerful outpouring of the Holy Spirit begins to understand how he will serve the Savior, sharing the blessed hope of salvation. Affliction produced endurance in Peter, and that endurance would certainly shape his ministry. That proven character would bring the light of the gospel to many people as the first Christians began to walk this new path of service, venturing out into a waiting world.

I believe one day we will know the whys behind our losses, but for now I must accept as I trust God with the knowing, that I am where He has placed me. The intricacies of His plan are not mine to know now. "The secret things belong to the Lord our God, but the things revealed belong to us and to our children forever, that they may follow all the words of this law." (Deuteronomy 29:29 NIV) Knowing may be in time, or in eternity, or after this life is completed.

Lord, I am thankful that You hold the understanding of secret things I'm not ready to know. I can trust You to bring hope out of affliction, in Your way, in Your time. May I continue to leave my steps forward to You as You direct my steps. In Jesus' Name, Amen.

Grief notes: Permanently closing your loved one's email can be another "good-bye" to deal with. There is less of a chance for phishing fraud by having all communication through your email address.

Journal 83

"Do not rejoice over me, my enemy! Though I have fallen, I will stand up; though I sit in darkness, the Lord will be my light." Micah 7:8

There are days. Those days when the Enemy brings thoughts across my path: you didn't do enough to help Dan. You should've been there when he passed. You could've insisted, pushed more. You failed him in his hour of need. And all of the what-ifs. What if I'd acted sooner? What if I could've gotten him in to another hospital? And so, it seems the Enemy rejoices to bring on the pain all over again, and once more I'm falling into a pit of guilt.

Guilt takes me down a rocky path of assumption that I could've orchestrated a different outcome as if I'd have been able to make the critical decisions with my own power. As if I could've done what God chose not to do. That responsibility doesn't belong to me, I realize now. That was God's timing and plan. I can't assign fault and blame as a burden to live with the rest of my life. Psalm 139:16 reminds me that all our days were written in His book and planned before we had lived our first day. No amount of guilt, fault-claiming or my own doing could change that.

"Though I have fallen, I will stand up; though I sit in darkness, the Lord will be my light." Regardless of what the Enemy tries to dredge up for his guilt attack, I know I can carry it all to the Lord, confess my feelings of guilt, and claim the forgiveness and peace that only He can give. He will be the light going forward. The light that guides through His Word, reminding me I don't have the final word on His Sovereign plan.

But what about real guilt and real regrets? What if there are unsettled issues that still gnaw at the heart? Unresolved questions can draw us into a tug of war with the enemy. 1John 1:9 holds true for those as well: "If we [freely] admit that we have sinned and confess our sins, He is faithful and just [true to His own nature and promises] and will forgive our sins and cleanse us continually from all unrighteousness [our wrongdoing, everything not in conformity with His will and purpose.]" (Amp) I can step out of that darkness where lies live and give it to God.

I will stand up. The Lord will be my light. I must trust that He wants me to let go of guilt and to heal from this pain of loss. I also know He wants me to learn from it. To learn more of His comfort so I can comfort others who are where I have been. To learn more of who He is, so I can continue trusting His leading through whatever He chooses, showing me new purpose in this life. But I know this: He's got my back when it comes to the Enemy attacks, and I am confident of how much He loves me. Zephaniah 3:17 says, "The Lord your God is with you, the Mighty Warrior who saves. He will take great delight in you; in His love he will no longer rebuke you but will rejoice over you with singing." (NIV) It may feel like darkness at the moment, but I know where the Light comes from.

Lord, Thank You, my protector, Jehovah Nissi. When the enemy brings guilt, I trust You to lift me up and give me peace. When the enemy brings darkness and despair, You bring light. When the Enemy leaves me weak with fear, I know that my strength comes from You. I praise You for all Your provision and help. In Jesus' Name, Amen

> **Grief notes: Old hymns often refer to Heaven and the grief we have in life. Spend some time perusing old hymnals. There are a lot of encouraging words to be found in the old-time songs of praise as well as comfort for the trials of life.**

Journal 84

"You will be delivered by returning and resting; your strength will be in quiet confidence." Isaiah 30:15

Returning and resting. The Israelites would return to their land after their exile, their long separation, and their strength would be found in their quiet confidence: that calm knowing, trusting that God was indeed with them, guiding, helping, and providing for them.

I take a deep breath, and make that conscious, intentional decision to seek Him for what is next. I peer down the corridor of the possible years ahead. I am returning and resting in what I know of God's sovereignty, His grace, and His provision, as well as His power to do what I could never do independently. And this is where I gain a new perspective: He can prepare me and use me in ways and areas I've never thought of yet. In the waiting, in the hurting, in the healing that seems to be a daily struggle, He gives me a fresh outlook: He holds the future, He has a reason for me to still be here, and Creator that He is, He can create opportunities I cannot even imagine now.

He delivers me from the enemy who prepares a pity party before in the presence of my doubts. He rescues me from the fears that tomorrow will be lonely, without hope, and barren of joy. He liberates me from the mindset of the captive that says I've already used up all the good that God has for me. But God has His plans. Instead, He promises a "crown of beauty instead of ashes, oil of joy instead of mourning, and a garment of praise instead of a spirit of despair." The world might think: what value is this one? She's a widow. She's just going to be a neediness drain on your friendship, your church, your community. Yet, that's not God's plan for me: "They will be called great oaks of righteousness, a planting of the Lord for the display of His splendor." (Isaiah 61: 3 NIV) A giant oak springs from a little acorn into a branching tower of strength and majesty where flocks of birds may rest, and even become a source of shade in the heat. There is hope for having a new purpose, to serve God on this new path in life, becoming a "planting of the Lord for the display of His splendor."

Daily I ask the Lord, "What's in store for today, Lord?" He is teaching me, step by step, to listen to His voice leading me. "Whether you turn to the right or to the left, your ears will hear a voice behind you, saying, 'this is the way, walk in it.'" (Isaiah 30:21 NIV) He will reveal all that He has for me. So comforting and reassuring when my strength is running low that "your strength will be in quiet confidence." In the quiet, in the calm, I know this: His grace always provides.

Lord, I am thankful for the quiet, peaceful confidence that I can face each tomorrow with because of You, Your Son, and the Holy Spirit. Your Sovereign grace provides what I cannot anticipate and prepares the way ahead as You lead me forward. There is not a tomorrow You have not seen, and no place that You do not accompany me. May I always return and rest in the quiet confidence of Your abiding strength. In Jesus' Name, Amen.

Grief notes: Commonplace books are another way to store thoughts, quotes, poems, letters, prayers, or notes on different topics. It's a way to compile and preserve various bits of information. They are different from a journal, as a journal usually consists of your own words, and is in chronological sequence. Creating a commonplace book on grief

might be another way to keep helpful quotes from books, copy some prayers, or jot down comforting thoughts that have helped you.

Journal 85

"For God has not given us a spirit of fear, but one of power, love and sound judgment." 2 Timothy 1:7

I keep trying to peek ahead, looking forward into this new journey for this year, next year, and onward, and this natural curiosity is tinged with some apprehension. How can I manage new life responsibilities on my own? (I haven't mown a lawn in a few years!) Will I be defeated by weariness and loneliness? (Going out to eat on my own is new territory!) Will I have to keep looking for a new purpose in life? (Wait…that's God's call…) Suddenly, I'm recognizing the enemy's fingerprint of fear. So just as quickly, I respond with a "Nope! That's not a spirit from God!"

The Spirit was given to us to bring power, love, and sound judgment "a calm, well-balanced mind and self-control" (AMP). Some days, the widow's fog clouds my thinking, but now I'm realizing what an amazing resource we have in the Holy Spirit! He knows our needs before we even ask.

Even in those moments when hope seems distant, and we feel powerless to step into doing "the next thing", we can re-read Romans 5:5, "Such hope [in God's promises] never disappoints us, because God's love has been abundantly poured out in our hearts through the Holy Spirit Who was given to us." (AMP) Widows are championed by God, so we don't have to be timid in asking! He will richly pour out His love and provision into our hearts and lives through working of the Holy Spirit.

Where else would I go for help except to the Lord?! He is generous with the wisdom and discernment I need, taking rogue thoughts captive, demolishing arguments, and God-opposing pretenses, making my thought life obedient to Christ (2 Corinthians 10:5) Surrendering this journey to Him, for all this new territory, I can see clearer the fear-traps and recognize them for what they are: distractions. I must remember trust is a choice. I will choose to trust His plan, His best for my life. What He has invested in me through His Holy Spirit, He knows I can do this journey, because He's provided for what He's called me to do.

So, despite what I may lack now, His rich fullness can work through my requests for today, and every tomorrow. Step by step, He will guide me to solutions for what the day requires and the gifts it holds in store. Meanwhile, He's providing power through confidence to learn new skills, sharing love by gifting me time with my kids and grandkids, and sound judgment by reminding me to rest when I need to stop and take a breather.

Holy Father, I am in awe that in Your infinite sovereign wisdom and grace, You gifted us Your Holy Spirit providing Power, Love, and Sound Judgment. You know widows need these. So, Lord, I surrender this path to You. Every Day. And I thank You for Your faithfulness, for I know I can trust You to guide me for every tomorrow. In Jesus' Name, Amen.

> **Grief notes: Memorizing scripture is good for the body and soul. Commit to memory the verses that inspire, comfort, and encourage you. It keeps your brain healthy, and it helps with spiritual warfare!**

Journal 86

"Whatever happens, conduct yourselves in
a manner worthy of the gospel of Christ."
Philippians 1:27

Lately I'm noticing that I just don't have enough mental "bandwidth" to deal with a lot of drama. Some folks seem intent on making small talk and comments, in manner or topics, that seem hard to process. In my heart and mind, I'm thinking this: those aren't things I care about anymore. I have just stopped watching or reading the news that unsettles me. I often have so much emotion swirling around inside me that adding one more disturbing story is just too much. My cup is full.

It would be easy to snap at those who don't understand that my cup is overflowing. Some folks seriously do not recognize that pouring out into an already-full cup brings a state of feeling overwhelmed. And sometimes I have to be honest and right up front and let them know that I can't deal with that topic or situation right now. In time, maybe, but not now. My head and my heart are processing a lot these days.

But then I read this verse: Whatever happens. Whatever situation I'm in and it may be one of those where I'm in a conversation with an unaware or insensitive person. Yes, I mixed up some words as I was talking, but you pointed it out, had a chuckle at my expense: "Did you hear what you just said?" Oh, Lord, I am thankful they can't hear how discombobulated my thinking really is! This widow's fog is a real and it rolls in like a Galilean Sea storm front. Yet this: Whatever happens, conduct myself, managing and controlling my behavior in a manner worthy of the gospel of Christ. My priority and my intention to serve Him first needs to be present, not my overwhelmed exasperation. Not a sharp, snippy, snarky comeback. I must remember grace. Remember to respond with grace.

Yes, whatever happens, it's my response that carries the biggest impact. Will my thoughtless response offend someone who has never talked with a widow new to her loss? That could've been me trying to converse with a widow before my own loss experience. That one stops me short: who have I offended? I need to remember this: I, too, need God's grace for my own replies. And in turn, remember that whatever happens, whatever conversations I find myself in, to recall that my response is what counts, because I need to reflect the gospel of Christ and how He is perceived. "Let the words of my mouth and the meditation of my heart be acceptable in Your sight, O Lord, my rock and my redeemer." (Psalm 19: 14 NIV)

Lord, I am thankful for Your grace so I can respond and behave toward others in a way that honors the name of Jesus. Whatever happens, may the "Words of my mouth and meditations of my heart" bring others to You to discover the One who loves them and died in their place to provide sin forgiveness, and a home in Heaven, for that is the Gospel I want my life to speak. In Jesus' name, Amen

Grief notes: Many folks agree that the second year of grief is harder. It's not the fresh pain of grief, and the fog is starting to lift, but the reality of the loss becomes painfully clearer.

Journal 87

"We do not know what to do, but we look
to You." 2 Chronicles 20:12

So many decisions, directions, needs, and tasks
present themselves these days. It used to be two people
working through these moments, these projects, and these
lists! Then I came upon Jehoshaphat's prayer. He realized
before whom he stood. "Lord…are You not the God Who
is in Heaven…Power and might are in Your hand, and no
one can stand against You." (2 Chronicles 20:6) And so he
enumerates their needs before God. But then he states this:
"We do not know what to do, but we look to You."

Oh, I can relate. I look at some tasks and I recognize
anew the loss of the one who helped me gather tax information, and all the paperwork and forms I'll have to wade
through solo this year. The words of Jeremiah 32:17 come
to mind, "Oh, Lord God! You Yourself made the heavens
and earth by Your great power and with Your outstretched
arm. Nothing is too difficult for You!" And that includes

putting together tax information. I must trust that the one who brought me this far will lead me on to the completion of this next challenge.

I love how the Lord replies to Jehoshaphat: "Do not be afraid or discouraged because of this vast number, for the battle is not yours, but God's." (v.15) In trust and relying on God's promises, like Jehoshaphat and Jeremiah, I know I'm in good company. Yet I see that the Lord can lead me through these battles. Well, they only seem like battles, as I have to strategize how to organize and march forward through the paperwork, the forms, the totaled sums and the marvelous patience of a tax preparer we had worked with for many years, stepping into the gap to provide a list of what I needed to simply send off in the mail to him. Yes, the Lord was making a way, where I could not imagine there was a way. After all, He declares that the battle is His! "Position yourselves, stand still, and see the salvation of the Lord…Do not be afraid or discouraged. Tomorrow, go out and face them, for the Lord is with you." (v.17)

The battle is His. Stand still. Don't be afraid or discouraged. The Lord is with you. Nothing is too difficult for Him. I may not know what to do, but God continues to provide His wisdom and a large dose of grace. I often realize I don't know what to do next, where to turn, how to proceed. But He does. The power and might for these days are in His faithful hands. And no one—-literally no one—can stand against Him. He provides. He knows what I need before I even ask. And again, He is the Source. The battle is His. Every time I turn to Him, casting all my cares on Him, I see the wonders of how He cares for me.

Lord, when life brings tasks my way that overwhelm me, I know I can look to You for help. Your strength upholds me, Your wisdom guides me, and Your grace sustains me. I know that nothing is too difficult for You. Thank you for leading me forward as I trust in You for faithfully providing answers. In Jesus' Name, Amen

> **Grief notes: Every day, and especially on the hard days, find the things that point you back to Christ. From reading to music choices, to what you watch on streaming TV, choose something that directs your thoughts to God to promote our healing.**

Journal 88

"Pay attention to the ministry you have received in the Lord, so that you can accomplish it." Colossians 4:17

One thing I'm learning: God's not finished with me. In fact, He's at work remodeling me and what my priorities are now. I can see there is still a purpose for me, and He has a ministry, a role of service, that He will reveal as a plan going forward. I'm also realizing this: my heart is in a different place because what used to be important has shifted. Granted, I was usually all about what Dan was planning, our next "thing". But now, I'm more aware of those who are hurting, quicker to feel the pain of someone who's lost a loved one. I want others to know that grief healing is only accomplished through the Lord, that only through the power of His Holy Spirit is there a deeper resource for walking on in this journey.

How do I pay attention to this calling on my life now? How can I steward this time of loss to bring the glory to

Christ? After all, without what He has done to comfort me, to bring peace and His presence into my pain of losing Dan, to walk with me through the ache of being separated at his last days by pandemic restriction, I would've been lost. How does anyone face these days without knowing the Lord and receiving strength from being able to trust in His plan?

"Pay attention to the ministry you have received in the Lord…" See to it that you complete the ministry you've received; the Apostle Paul gives these instructions to pass along to Archippus, one of the pastors in Colossae. Yes, I know what our goals were then as a couple in seeking the Lord and living for Him, so how do I as a widow walk out goals and priorities in a new life calling? Honestly, I am so thankful I knew the Lord for many years before this season, but this, like no other experience has brought a deeper trust in my Savior. He gave peace when I asked, He brought strength at my weakest point, He surrounded me with comfort like nothing else when feeling the amputation of "my other half" ripped from me. The Lord's presence was there in His Word, in my deep spirit-groaned prayers. And like nothing else, I want others to know that they, too, can access this peace, comfort, and strength as well.

"So that you can accomplish it…" To put this experience of loss to use as a stewardship of what the Lord has provided, like stewarding our time for Him, our talents for His Name, or the use of our "treasure", my priority now is to share Jesus daily. My purpose for each day as I wake up is to ask the Lord: Where can I share You with others today? And really, I'm discovering that "purpose" is not a grand overarching marquee that will be a one-time great revelation in lights and fireworks. It's simply every day giving our day back to the Lord to do His work, to say yes when He prompts me to serve. (I'm going to the store, Lord. Show me how you want me to share Jesus.)

Yes, I must "pay attention" to this new purpose, in this new season, so I can accomplish what He's calling me to do.

Lord, Thank You for the opportunities You give to share with others who need to know Your plan of salvation, who need to know Your peace and strength, and above all, who need to know Your power to heal their broken hearts and spirits. Jesus, you felt the loss and separation from Your Father when You hung on the cross for our sins. Lead me to souls today who need You, open hearts that need You, as I find purpose going forward serving You. In Jesus' Name, Amen.

Grief notes: Find a Christian group who understands grief, especially a widow's grief. GriefShare is a good place to start. Some churches have a Stand In the Gap for Widows ministry. Seek one or start one if you can, as this is a need in many churches. Being with those who have or are experiencing similar losses allows you to process your loss on a level like no other. There is a more complete understanding and connection.

Journal 89

"You will go out with joy and be led forth in peace; the mountains and the hills will burst into song before you, and all the trees of the field will clap their hands." Isaiah 55:12

Tuesday it rained. All day, mind you. I'm discovering that a Central Texas downpour is not like an Oregon drizzle. Yet the rain was so needed here to bring about the seeds' germination, young buds, and bringing signs of the green hope of Spring.

I think about the signs of hope in grief. Realizing that God still has a plan for my life revives hope in me. Where the rain of tears still falls at times, I am finding they are healing moments, not to be denied. They simply honor Dan. And through these moments, I am beginning to see the promise of God's purpose through the greening mountains, hills in bloom, and even the brightening fields: "You will go out with joy and be led forth in peace". There is a restoration of hope, a newness of life, and a fresh calling on my life for this day.

In Christ, I have His joy and peace to share with others who need that good news in their lives. For some, they need the hope I've found in Him, as there is no other hope like His living, eternal hope.

"The mountains and the hills will burst into song before you." What a picture that paints! Mountains and hills bursting with color that only our Creator could make. And yet, I'm reminded that where there are mountains and hills, there are also valleys, dark valleys through the shadow of death and loss. But He promised to be with us, that we need not fear evil, for He is Lord of mountains and hills bursting with melody, yet He also has a song for the dark night that may envelop us. And others need to hear that music that comes straight from the Father's heart to comfort and reassure us that He's still here, and as Philippians 1:6 says, "He who began a good work in us will complete it." Our purpose is His promise.

"And the trees of the field will clap their hands" shows us that although grief may prune us and change us, our Heavenly Father, our Creator God continues to craft the blossoms for each season of renewal and provides new ways we can serve and celebrate all He has done for us. The cropping and clipping we've undergone at the Master Gardener's hands shows His design for the new ways we will yet serve Him. My hope is that in these life changes, I continue to yield to His call on my life.

So as the rain comes, may I look beyond the gray skies and the mud, to see the hope in the joy and peace I can share with others who may be looking for and needing what only Christ can bring forth.

Lord, I see the hope that is in You alone, the hope for real joy and peace that is only found in Your Son, Jesus. Lead me today to share this message with someone who is in the Dark Valley, needing the strength to continue, despairing of ever seeing the hope of the mountain top. Let me share Your hope. In Jesus' Name, Amen.

> **Grief notes: You need help. Every widow does, as we are tackling tasks that used to be our beloved's jobs. Finding help can be a project, but some churches do have community boards for services or life groups focused on being "helping hands". Even Facebook usually has a local community page for asking who will mow lawns in your area. Seek, and you may find new friends waiting to help!**

Journal 90

"Don't throw away your confidence, which has a great reward. For you need endurance, so that after you have done God's will, you may receive what was promised."
Hebrews 10:35-36

Some mornings—who am I kidding—most mornings, I wake up thinking: Groundhog's Day. This is how every day will be from now on, forever, until I go to heaven. And in that moment, I have to make a choice: Do I trust the Lord enough to say: This is His best for me for now until eternity? Can I run this race with endurance? (But first, I may need to take captive some Enemy deception influencing my thoughts!)

God has given me a challenge in this new season: Will you trust Me? I've walked with Him for many years, trusting Him to meet needs, heal sick kids, provide answers, keep us safe, and for thousands of miles of traveling mercies. But now, when it's me, just me, it's heavy lifting in my asking for strength when there's disappointment, for grace when it's a heart-heavy day, or for wisdom when there are choices before me. So, I take a moment to remember that this is all His strength, this is His grace, and this is His wisdom, and trusting Him is my confidence, my bold, confident trust in what He can and will do. "Don't throw away your confidence…" I hang on to my faith that sadness is temporary, but the Lord's provisions are eternal. I am keeping my focus on the many ways He has met my needs, comforted me, given me strength and grace and that comes with great reward. So, yes, my confidence is planted in Him. Hebrews 10:23 says, "Let us hold fast the confession of our hope without wavering for He Who promised is faithful."

"For you need endurance…" It's morning after morning, realizing again and again, this is the new path I'm trusting to His guiding. With His strength, wisdom, and grace, He is teaching me endurance. And endurance makes me stronger. Like Monday morning doing my two-mile tread-mill workup, I'd like to stop after mile one! But no, it won't feel any better on Tuesday or Wednesday! Keep going! I know the leg-weight machines will go better after the warmup! Same with the endurance the Lord wants me to work on. Keep going. Follow the purpose He's placing on my heart. Reach out, step out, send a text, make that call, drop a note. Stay in community. Find ways to serve. He's building my stamina.

Building endurance in the grief journey is not to deny grief. Laying the groundwork for this new life started when I first recognized that Sovereign God has a plan. Romans 5: 3-4 reminds us that suffering, and troubles helps us build endurance, and that ends up taking us through perseverance, character building, and hope. And that's what it's all about: hope. The Lord wants me to be a person of hope for others who need Him. And this: that my confidence in His endurance-building brings me to His purpose for my life going forward and that is to share the hope of Christ with others who need Him.

Lord, Thank You for the daily strength that comes from You, that I can have bold confident trust that what comes my way and it is ordained by You. Lead me today to those who need You. Guide my thoughts, direct my steps, and may I go in Your strength. In Jesus' Name, Amen.

Grief notes: Prayer is so important in the grieving process. In the early days, it was a heart cry for the pain and sorrow. As

we turn our needs to the Lord, He provides, and we thank Him. This builds our faith. We find He is truly faithful, the Champion of widows and Father to our fatherless children. He also wants us to seek His ways. He also delights when we ask how we can serve Him. Always pray.

Journal 91

> "By faith Abraham, when he was called,
> obeyed and set out for a place that he was
> going to receive as an inheritance. He went
> out, even though he didn't know where he
> was going." Hebrews 11:8

God told Abraham to "Go", so he pulled up tent pegs, loaded up all he owned, along with his wife, servants, and his nephew. And he left, even though he had no idea where they were going. Simple obedience to God's call on His life: I will bless you. But there was an inheritance ahead. So, Abraham left. That's trust, and that's faith.

As they journeyed, nothing looked familiar to him, I'm sure. He'd never been this way before; it was all new territory. He just went as the Lord had told him. "Over there, that's the land your children will own one day," this special encounter with God here at the oak of Moreh made such an impression that he built an altar to the Lord. On to the hill country the Lord led these travelers, and he pitched his tent within sight of two cities, but again, he built an altar to Lord and called on the name of the One who led him. So, on he went, in stages along the path the Lord was leading. Listening to the One who'd called him, building places to worship Him along the way, all the while having faith that although this route was not easy, He could trust God's word, and endure whatever lie before him. He was content to be a temporary resident, seeing from a distance what would someday be his because he trusted Him who led.

Starting out on this journey of widowhood, I can see how God is asking me to rely on Him. Like Abraham, I've never traveled this route before. Nothing is familiar, except the Lord's voice leading me as He's promised. Tent pegs packed away, nothing looks like home, but I notice there's community here where He's led, fellowship, and others who grieve. There's also quiet and space to rest. Here is where I can find a spot to pitch my tent. A place to worship. To spend time with family, reminding them that only one thing is important and that is to be ready for eternity. Yes, I'll follow where He leads, serve where He directs, and find joy in this journey, for there's Heaven ahead. Grief, yes, it follows. But when James says count it all joy when you fall into trials, because those hard trials produce endurance, and that endurance has to finish its course so I can be complete in this life, and I must be ready to give that glory of completion one day to Jesus. After all, He is my strength to endure.

So, I will look for places along this journey where I can stop and worship Him for all He has done and is doing. This is a call on my life, this loss. God's calling me to go along a path I've never been on. I know along this way that He will reveal purposes for me that only He knows. And every day it requires my yes.

Lord, I surrender to You as I learn to trust Your way, and obey Your voice as guided by Your Word. May I like Abraham be content to daily move my tent to seek each new purpose You have for me for I know the wonders of Heaven lie ahead for eternity. In Jesus' Name, Amen

> **Grief notes: If you have older children with their own families, don't expect that they will automatically know what you need. As you own that this is your new life, you will begin to make new friends and connections at church or in your community. Remember that your family is likely still in their own grief and grieving is not**

just your own burden. Find ways to honor your beloved together with a favorite meal or activity he would've enjoyed.

Journal 92

"…that you may know the way by which
you must go, for you have not passed this
way before." Joshua 3:4

I turned north onto I-35 and the thought hit me at
once: I've never driven on this stretch of freeway! Overpasses
that arched against the Central Texas sky, soon gave way to
strip malls, busy clover leafs, and worst of all the dreaded
sea of road construction. Even the GPS was unsure of my
destination now as it recalculated continuously through the
orange cone jungle. I am a stranger in a strange land.

Joshua was given instructions not to "turn to the right,
nor to the left, so you'll have success wherever you go."
(Joshua 1:7. He was to study these directions, meditate
on them, and carefully observe each detail. God gives the
greatest secret in verse 9: "Haven't I commanded you to be
strong and courageous? Do not be afraid or discouraged,
for the Lord your God is with you wherever you go." No,
not Joshua's own courage and strength, but the almighty

Angel-army God's own presence would be reinforcing every step and effort!

But then, it was go-time. God's presence, the Ark of the Covenant, would go before them first, they would follow at a bit of distance. There was to be enough room so the travelers could see the way to go. "For you have never been this way before."

These would be cautiously courageous steps. You know those first steps we take early in grief. Those things that must get done. Burial arrangements. Life insurance. Death certificates. Those are raw days starting out on this journey. All new steps, changing forever how things get done. Not we, but I. Yet the presence of God, leading my feet to trust these tentative new steps, weak ankles on different slopes and always the focus: Don't be afraid. For the Lord your God is with you wherever you go. And sometimes I'd stand on that promise for a while, catching a ragged breath. Venturing on, I'd be reminded that His grace was enough because His strength is made perfect in my weakness. And trying out my casting abilities, I'd cast all my cares (fears, worries, sadness) on Him because He cares for me. Each realization of how well He'd brought peace and comfort to the table prepared before me caused my trust to deepen and my ankles to strengthen on this new pathway He's called me to.

Just to see the Jordan drawing back the waters, and safe passage being mine, I don't need to wonder if God can do this. God is doing this. Mightily! And I want to grab some memorial stones, stones that will be reminders to my children and grandchildren yet to come: God did this. God can. I want to echo what the people spoke to Joshua: "Everything you have commanded, we will do, and everywhere you send us, we will go." (Joshua 1:16). I recognize whose marching orders these are.

Lord, I am thankful that where You lead comes with Your presence right here beside me and going before me. I want to honor You with my obedience, even when I must step out onto painful new territories. In Jesus' Name, Amen

> **Grief notes: Surrender this passage to God. Let Him know all is His: the pain, the missing, the frustration, the lonely times, the solo journeys we drive, the special days. Wrap them in your trust and lay them before Him. He will take them and, in their place, Himself.**

> "But the jar that he was making from the clay became flawed in the potter's hand, so he made it into another jar, as it seemed right for him to do." Jeremiah 18:4

So little recognizable remains of what used to be my life. There's been an adjusting of what I do, how I live, and learning to navigate as a widow. There's been a reset, it seems, to everything except for God, and He remains faithful, reliable, unchanging. I know that He is there for me in every moment.

God sent Jeremiah to observe a potter working with clay on a wheel since He knew exactly what Jeremiah would see upon his arrival. This was imagery that would serve to remind Israel of how Almighty God can form, and reform our lives in so many ways. As he is watching the potter, the jar he was creating became flawed, so he just threw it all in the trash? No, quite the opposite! Jeremiah watched as the potter skillfully turned and fashioned the clay into a new jar! "As it seemed right for him to do," the Word states. Yes, the jar had not yet been fired in a kiln, a step what would have meant the jar had been completed, as the firing process changes the chemical make-up of the clay, removing the water that can't be replaced. There was hope for that jar in the hands of the potter to be designed anew with a new purpose, perhaps.

And so it is with a widow's life. God's work isn't completed in me yet. There's some transforming going on. What was, is no longer what He needs me to be, so I am back on the Potter's wheel where His hands are redesigning me for His next purpose. As the Potter crushes and reforms the clay into the new jar, I think of the weeks and months since Dan's home-going, and all the ways God's hand has been directing, tenderly here, firmly there, upholding, and a gentle press along the way as He guides toward new plans for me. Likely, this will be the process until my own home-going, until He says, Complete.

That reminds me that there is still hope. Like new purposes type of hope. Some days it may seem like there's nothing more, but God is still on the throne, the Potter is still at the wheel. Even if this jar gets ruined, marred, flawed in the turning, in the Creator's hands, He still can make all things new. Leaning into His Almighty crafting plans, He knows the future as well as He knows the past and every jar and pot He's ever turned. Psalm 103:14 says, "For He knows how we are formed, He remembers that we are dust." He knows us, but more than that, He loves us, these jars of clay, and wants us to be useful for Him until that day He says—done.

Lord, You are the Potter and I am the clay in Your hands. This reshaping is not easy, but I know You have a plan and will design me for where I can serve You best. May I yield to the reforming process and surrender to Your Master Plan. In Jesus' Name, Amen.

> **Grief notes: Joy isn't the emotion of happiness, but it is a constant contentment that we can know and trust the Lord. It's worth the struggle to keep moving forward in our healing because we have a constant experience of faith that He is faithful, and He is in control.**

Journal 94

"Endure suffering as discipline...no discipline seems enjoyable at the time, but painful. Later on, however, it yields the peaceful fruits of righteousness to those who have been trained by it." Hebrews 12:7, 11

Diets, exercise programs, and completing projects, all require self-control and a firm hand on how I spend my time, where my thinking goes, and having to say no to some things for the greater good of a goal. I'm beginning to understand how suffering through the loss of Dan, this grief journey, is a sort of discipline. It's not enjoyable, and sometimes it's downright painful. But if this is, as I believe, a suffering that God has called me to endure, I can trust there's good in it for me somewhere, sometime.

James 1:2 says, "Consider it a great joy...whenever you experience various trials." At first glance, that's a hard thought for a grieving widow, but God designed this trial. There is something in me He wants to perfect, so the first choice I make is to trust. Like the first day at the gym, you know all those screaming muscles that need help, so if you endure the discipline, and every week you get stronger. Similarly, if I trust my needs, my worries, and my loss to the Lord, I can also trust Him with endurance. He is powerful enough to handle it all. He can provide. His faithful promises have proven true time and time again. I can see He has a plan for me, and still there is a plan that remains for my life.

There are ambushes in any discipline: sickness, busyness, and needs of others can interrupt the patterns of life. Holiday overindulgence might derail the best diet plan. However, Anniversaries and milestones of memory will come along and shake my resolve to endure this new journey of grief. But according to James 1: 12, "Blessed is the one who endures trials, because when he has stood the test he will receive the crown of life..." A crown of life. That is something valuable I can lay at the feet of Jesus as a thank You for all He has done for me. I will continue to believe in faith that this is my Father's best.

Endurance has a reward. When I can see that God has been so faithful in this season of transition, fulfilling promises of comfort, provision, peace, and strength, I can't help but notice: I am changing. And I can appreciate in James 1:4 where it says, "Let endurance have its full effect, so that you may be mature and complete, lacking nothing." My faith is not what it was. I can tell God's training along this path is bringing about those peaceable fruits of His Righteousness He's been cultivating. There's so much to remind myself about enduring on this path, yet I can see where the Lord is training and strengthening me. Philippians 2: 13 says, "For it is God Who is working in you both to will and to work according to His good purpose." And there it is: He's training me for His good purpose.

Lord, Thank You for coaching me through this training. Your sufficient grace is reinforcing my weakness with Your perfect strength. My endurance comes from casting it all daily on You. In Jesus' Name, Amen.

> **Grief notes: Grieving can sometimes make other losses surface that perhaps still need some healing. Be patient with yourself as you examine other losses experienced earlier in life. Bring this loss to the Lord as well and seek a renewed healing.**

Journal 95

"May our Lord Jesus Christ Himself and God our Father, Who has loved us and given us eternal encouragement and good hope by grace, encourage your hearts and strengthen you in every good work and word." 2 Thessalonians 2:16-17

As I near the one-year anniversary of Dan going to Heaven, I'll admit that there are still some days where it's like lead boots on the floor to get up in the morning. Some days can still be tinged with recalling loss, and I'm tempted to pull back into a shell and feel the burden of time. So again, I call a stop in those dreary tracks: Lord, You have pulled me through worse mornings than this. It's me again, and I'm in need of Your strength, Your comfort, and Your peace.

Suddenly I'm recalling all the blessings that have come my way since Dan went to Heaven. I consider all the ways the Lord has carried me, comforted me, and brought answers to long standing prayers. The unique opportunities He's brought me to share my hope in Jesus, and provisions that came only from Him. Then I read this verse: "Who has loved us and given us eternal encouragement and good hope by grace." His love that never fails, a supply of encouragement that is unending and good, firm, confident hope as well as my salvation in Him, by grace. God wants me to move forward, following Him and His encouragement. He is bringing healing, layer upon layer, like new skin on a wound is this hope He's giving.

I see that His strength is surrounding me, indwelling me, reminding me that He is all, everything I need. When I start trying to drive forward, I can't be looking in the rearview mirror. He prompts me to remember this is a new path, His new purpose. His encouragement shows me that I must trust Him to leave the old to venture into the new. Like Joshua could not stay on the other side of the Jordan and still be the leader God called him to be. Ruth couldn't stay in Moab and still reap the blessings that awaited in Bethlehem. Zacchaeus couldn't stay up the tree and still have dinner with Jesus. So for me, I can't keep longing for yesterday's normal and still go where God now intends for me to go.

"May the Lord Jesus Christ Himself and God our Father … encourage your hearts and strengthen you in every good work and word." This promise of help along the new path is the ultimate roadside assistance. He knows we'll have days when we'll call for help, and He'll graciously bring encouragement, good hope, and strength. He knows the way I am to go and will lead through in the manner He has planned. Psalm 37:23-24 says, "A person's steps are established by the Lord, and He takes pleasure in his way. Though he falls, he will not be overwhelmed, because the Lord supports him with His hand." That has been so reassuring to me on this widow's pathway. The Lord is near, and He supports me, forever! That's eternal encouragement. This is healing.

Lord, Your eternal encouragement gives me strength and hope. I'm thankful that You called me into a new life to serve. I know Your presence will guide and support in every good work. In Jesus' Name, Amen

> **Grief notes: Simplifying your life is important as you grieve. Stress will make you more anxious and can cause its own issues. Try not to overbook your days even if you are trying to socialize more. Approach your activities with a plan that if it becomes too much for you, you can leave at any time. Remember that working on grief takes up a lot of your energy.**

Journal 96

"And let the peace of Christ…rule in your hearts." Colossians 3:15

Oh, the thieves of peace. They have a way of sneaking into life and making you think they are the game-changers. Like it's their call whether this day, this need, this next valley is going to be a problem. It's not their say, but I need to recall the shenanigans these peace-thieves will try.

Fear. They will try to make me believe there's no hope for tomorrow. Concern that I won't have enough time, energy, strength, or money to meet future needs. That panic that everything is on my shoulders. But then Philippians 4:6-7 reminds me to not be anxious about anything but pray about everything. "And the peace of God…will guard your hearts and minds in Christ Jesus."

Overwhelmed. Yes, some days the "overwhelm" hits me. There may be too many decisions to make all at once. The unexpected leak in the ceiling, the one-more-thing and suddenly, the thief of peace is circling me, prowling for my weakest moment. Jesus gave wise advice in Matthew 11:28, "Come to me, all of you who are weary and carry heavy burdens, and I will give you rest." And again, in Matthew 19:26, "…with men this is impossible; but with God all things are possible." I Peter 5:7 also reminds us to "Cast all your cares (anxieties) on Him, for He cares for you."

I can't go back and change a thing about this new transition I'm in, but regret is yet another peace thief. This can be tricky especially if it relates to our late husband. What I should have done, ways I could have acted, or even memories of how I could've been a better wife, all sneak in to steal my peace. And once more, I take those thoughts prisoner through Jesus. I must accept what was: the events and every detail. Again Psalm 139:16 comes to mind: "All my days were written in Your book and planned before a single one of them began." Written and planned. Every step, every detail, God knew, designed, and planned. And God was fully there, even when I could not be present with him. So, no, I cannot give up my peace to a peace-thief that wants to override God's sovereign plan. It's happened before, and I know where to take that thinking every time that bandit tries to rob my peace of heart and mind with regrets.

So, I must let the peace of God rule in my heart. That word "rule" means to umpire or to call the decisions. I choose the calm within that He gives when I'm walking with Him, letting Him be the controlling, deciding factor in my heart, settling questions as they arise. When fear tries to steal my peace, or being overwhelmed marks my day, or that old guilt and regret raise their heads, I know who these scoundrels are! They are the thieves of my peace. Most importantly, I know they are from the Enemy of my soul.

Yes, taking our hearts back from the peace thieves is in God's hands. Isaiah 26:3 says, "You will keep in perfect peace all who trust in You, all whose thoughts are fixed on you." (NLT) And in John 16:33 Jesus says, "I have told you these things, so that in Me you may have peace. In this world, you will have trouble. But take heart! I have overcome the world." He is the one ruling with peace in our hearts! I don't want or need the Enemy's distraction of being drawn into peace thievery.

Lord, Your peace is not as the world gives, but we have a deep abiding peace that passes understanding. Help me to spot these peace thieves and keep Your peace ruling in my heart. In Jesus' Name, Amen

Grief notes: Grief creates a new tenderness surrounding family milestones. Grandchildren's birthdays, graduations, celebrations all make us aware of our beloved's absence. Keep their memory present by doing, or making something he would've created or mentioning something he might have said or he would've enjoyed on such an occasion.

"Elisha said, 'Don't be afraid, for those who are with us outnumber those who are with them'…So the Lord opened the servants' eyes, and he saw that the mountain was covered with horses and chariots of fire all around Elisha." 2 Kings 6:16-17

The enemy of our soul likes nothing better than to launch an attack upon a victim. He wants to deceive us and trick us into hopelessness. It's like the scene facing Elisha's servant early one morning as he stepped out of his door: the city was surrounded by horses, chariots, and an enemy army! Any hope of escape looked dim. You can hear the fear in his voice! The servant was rightfully shaken as he reported to Elisha, "Oh my master, what are we to do?!"

Yes, I've been there. I'm thinking, you, too, know that feeling. The army, the horses, the chariots all seem arrayed to win the day. "Oh, my master, what are we to do!"

Elisha was undisturbed at this. He didn't run out there shaking his fist at the troops. He didn't minimize the servant's alarm. His concern was for the faith of his servant. He wanted his servant to see what he knew about the Lord's support, and strength, and how the Almighty God fights battles. "Then Elisha prayed, 'Lord, please open his eyes and let him see.' So, the Lord opened the servant's eyes, and he saw that the mountain was covered with horses and chariots of fire all around Elisha." God's almighty army was revealed to the servant. There was protection, power, and proof that the enemy was outnumbered.

The servant's opened eyes did more for his faith than a 45-minute sermon on "Don't give up" or "God knows all about it" topics. He saw what the enemy army didn't see behind them. He saw what strengthened Elisha and gave him hope. And now that assurance and strength were his, too.

I'm thankful that God is still revealing hope through His almighty protection and power. Whether it's making a way through or around the troubles we face, we can trust that His presence is going with us and before us. Since victory over sin and death has already been declared through His Son, Jesus, and the Holy Spirit indwells every believer, those horses and chariots of fire surround us, too! The hundreds of promises in His Word remind us that His grace is sufficient, and His strength is made perfect in our weakness. He is our true Defender!

When I dive into His Word and abide in scriptures that call to mind Who this God is that we serve, it's as if Elisha has a hand on my shoulder and with the sound of the Enemy closing in, I can call to mind this: "Don't be afraid, for those who are with us outnumber those who are with them." And then God opens my eyes…again. I'm surrounded by His strength, His wisdom, and His grace. What deep peace.

Lord, When I am losing hope, open my eyes of faith to see that You are still my Defender, my Provider, and my Keeper. Thank You for Your deep peace in my troubled times. In Jesus' Name, Amen.

> **Grief notes: If there is an upcoming day that you feel sure will trigger you, ask a trusted friend to be in prayer for you. The person who says they are praying for you, this may be the one to ask for this special request.**

Journal 98

"But the Lord is faithful, and He will strengthen you [setting you on a firm foundation] and will protect and guard you from the evil one." 2 Thessalonians 3:3 (AMP)

The Central Texas storm warnings had been posted for two days: be prepared for wind, and damaging hail, as well as possible tornado activity. Plan ahead and be protected. Find shelter as this includes all humans, livestock, and property. I check out the local area meteorology radar maps and see where this system is coming from and where it's headed next.

This reminds me of the healing process of grief. When the storms and surges of heartache pass through, and it seems they roll through with each new realization of another loss incurred with Dan's passing, it seems the only advance preparation is knowing more of God. Reminding myself of who He is and hiding the Word in my heart are the only ways to keep me anchored. I try to recall the 30,000-foot view of where this loss came from, and how this pathway will move forward with God's plan and purpose. If I stay "ground level" and try to imagine tomorrow, I cannot see clearly. What I see: the unpacking of another storage tub and finding mementos of our life together; opening a box that contains his favorite t-shirts; sorting through his well-worn hand tools to find the wrench I need for the stubborn faucet. It's a vacuum force that can pull me to sadness and loss of real sight. What I see in God's timing: He is Sovereign, All-knowing, faithful, trustworthy, and Almighty. Just as His Word says. I take the time to thank Him for the years I had with Dan and remember this is just a pause before I see him again, that there is a path before me that is as clear to Him as that weather map. I know I can trust Him for the rest of the journey because He knows exactly what He's doing and where this path is going.

Yes, the Lord is and has been a faithful Champion, and continues to provide strength when I need it most. He sets me on a firm foundation, found only in Him. He will protect and guard from the evil one, the Enemy who wants nothing more than to discourage me and keep me in despair, whispering lies that challenge my belief and trust, and seeking to distract me in the pursuit of His purpose. This enemy wants us to believe we are alone, but if we have done our preparation for the resistance he brings, we can shelter in the Word of God as the storms rage.

Knowing scripture, having it hidden in my heart, has been a life saver. These verses that remind me that God is faithful (1 Corinthians 1:9), that He is my shelter (Psalm 46: 1-2) and a refuge and strength, a helper always found in times of trouble and that His peace will guard my heart and mind (Philippians 4:7). I can recall the scriptures that tell me that He is my protection, (Psalm 3:3) because He is a shield and the One Who lifts my head! So, no matter what appears on the Radar, I know I'm safe, hidden in Him, as His promises are tucked away in my heart.

Lord, I know the storms of life will come, but with Your promises, I can rest with confidence knowing You see me, You will be with me, and Your Almighty, guiding hand will protect. In Jesus' Name, Amen.

Grief notes: Having an illness or surgery after losing our beloved can be doubly hard. We miss their comforting love and care like none other. Take some time to give thanks for all the ways they were your

companion and source of help. These are new days in a new season and remember that God is with you always. He will provide the support we need.

Journal 99

"Keep your life free from the love of money. Be satisfied with what you have, for He Himself has said 'I will never leave you or abandon you.' Therefore, we may boldly say, 'The Lord is my helper, I will not be afraid'." Hebrews 13:5,6

Be satisfied. So many folks think satisfaction is never having to worry about money. As widows, we know too well the challenges of going from two to one person in the home. And now, to focus on a new purpose God has for my life, where will that help come from? How will I know?

Sometimes on our new pathway, we may struggle staying on track with what God's called us to do. We might get side-tracked and drawn off-course. We might begin looking too far into the future and get discouraged. It might be an over-loaded plate that disheartens us. Sometimes we sit and look at all the possibilities and feel overwhelmed, so we get side-lined. Other times, there are people speaking into our life that have other goals, and our purpose for Christ is not one of them. There are so many ways that we can get derailed from our purpose for the Lord.

Our purpose for the Lord is still there! God's special work for me is still where He will lead! Paul says it so well in this scripture from Hebrews: Remain satisfied with what you have. Be content. Above and beyond all other calls that come on your life, we have Christ helping us. We need to sit quietly with Him and listen for His voice in His Word and in the day to day as He brings those words to mind. He will never leave or abandon us. He won't mislead us! Does the call to serve seem difficult? "Therefore (that's why) we can boldly say, 'The Lord is my helper, I will not be afraid…'." Is the Lord showing you an opportunity? He will provide what you need to strengthen and prepare you for the task ahead. We can say confidently and courageously that the Lord is our helper!

Before Jesus returned to Heaven, He told the disciples that He would send the Holy Spirit. "And I will ask the Father, and He will give you another Helper [Comforter, Advocate, Intercessor, Counselor, Strengthener, Standby], to be with you forever." (John 14:16 Amp) What an amazing Heavenly Resource is with us as we step out with confident faith, trusting that where God leads, He provides the support we need.

As with every new turn in this journey, I will pray for wisdom and guidance about my steps forward. For today and every day, I will ask God to show me, lead me, and direct me. He can open and close doors, send me on a new path, and begin equipping me for other purposes He has up ahead. Above all, I am to trust Him. This season is from Him. He's carried me this far, and His faithful presence has never left me wondering or wandering. I will seek to be content. The Champion of widows is the Champion of this new path.

Lord, may I remain content with what I have, knowing that Your Holy Spirit will lead along this path of this new plan for my life, in Your timing, in Your way. I leave it in Your hands. In Jesus' Name, Amen.

> **Grief notes: After the loss of our beloved, making decisions can be hard as we were likely discussing options together and what would be best. We relied on his expertise and experience, but now things have changed. Where do we go? Do online research, ask others, find friends or family**

you trust to give an honest recommendation. Take your need for information to the Lord in prayer, asking for guidance and wisdom. When you decide, step out in faith, and leave your choice with God.

Journal 100

"Now to Him who is able to protect you
from stumbling and to make you stand in
the presence of His glory, without blemish
and with great joy, to the only God our
Savior, through Jesus Christ our Lord,
be glory, majesty, power and authority
before all time, now and forever. Amen."
Jude 1: 24-25

Sometimes saying "Thank You" is just not enough.
I search out the best card messages; I wrack my brain for
a thankful gesture to convey how grateful I am for someone's thoughtfulness. An immediate text of Thanks is not
enough, so I select my wording that reflects "I couldn't have
done this without you." I certainly could not have done this
journey without my Savior. I want my life to reflect a thank
You to my Lord.

So how do I thank the Almighty, Sovereign God who
has led me, comforted me, been my strength, been my

peace, and never left me? He is the only One who can keep me from stumbling on this new pathway and make me stand before Himself one day with great joy. He knows how difficult this journey is, has been, and will be. I remember, He knows my needs before I even ask, and He's able to bless beyond all I could ask or think. This Lord who was my very breath those first raw days of loss, gave help when I asked because I could not even imagine life. He gave me strength when my knees buckled. He made ways where I had no idea which way to go and I now realize that path had started long before I even became a widow. God was working way back then. In fact, He's always working.

So, what do I give as a thank You? Glory. Heavenly praise and honor that reflect to God how amazing He is, and how marvelous is His grace, strength, and wisdom. He gave the "road in the wilderness, rivers in the desert." (Isaiah 43:19) The wonders of how faithful promises in His Word reinforced my faith and my "weak ankles" on the mountain slopes rising from the dark valleys. Yes, it was Him, all Him. All thanks to Him.

In Matthew 5:16, Jesus said that those who believe are the lights of the world, so don't put a basket over the light, rather put that light on a lampstand so everyone can see. "In the same way, let your light shine before men so that they may see your good works, and give glory to your Father in heaven." When I begin to see that being a widow can be a way to shine for Him, God can use me. And because others hear that there is hope, and strength in Him, others will find Him because we are lighting the way to Him. And that brings glory to our Father in Heaven. A Heavenly thanks.

I want to remember to be thankful for each purpose or task He brings my way. I know there are lessons to learn and there is wisdom to gain. After all, this is a different route I'm now traveling. Unexpected for me, completely anticipated by Him. And one day I will be able to thank Him in person.

Lord, I praise You for the marvelous ways You care for me on this widow journey. You deserve all the Glory and Honor for I could never have done it without You. In Jesus' Name, Amen

Grief notes: Eating alone can be a challenge for the widow. As part of our grief, we may have lost our appetite and food preparation may have lost its appeal. Eating to be healthy is still important, but eating alone at home or out can be hard. Know someone who is also a widow?

Consider getting together to share a meal. Meal prepping for a few days might inspire you to eat right if you don't have to face the kitchen alone every night. Know a single mom who would appreciate a homemade meal? Serve her needs and you may find a new meal partner!